Preparing to Lead in a Digital Environment

Preparing to Lead in a Digital Environment

What All Educators Need to Know

Edited by
Lin Carver and Holly S. Atkins

ROWMAN & LITTLEFIELD
Lanham • Boulder • New York • London

Published by Rowman & Littlefield
An imprint of The Rowman & Littlefield Publishing Group, Inc.
4501 Forbes Boulevard, Suite 200, Lanham, Maryland 20706
www.rowman.com

6 Tinworth Street, London SE11 5AL, United Kingdom

British Library Cataloguing in Publication Information Available

Library of Congress Cataloging-in-Publication Data

Names: Carver, Lin, 1955- editor. | Atkins, Holly S., 1958- editor.
Title: Preparing to lead in a digital environment : what all educators need to know / edited by Lin Carver, Holly S. Atkins.
Description: Lanham : Rowman & Littlefield, [2021] | Includes bibliographical references and index. | Summary: "The book focuses on effective technology use and diffusion"—Provided by publisher.
Identifiers: LCCN 2020044091 (print) | LCCN 2020044092 (ebook) | ISBN 9781475858976 (cloth) | ISBN 9781475858983 (paperback) | ISBN 9781475858990 (epub)
Subjects: LCSH: Educational leadership—Data processing. | Education—Effect of technological innovations on.
Classification: LCC LB2806.17 .P74 2021 (print) | LCC LB2806.17 (ebook) | DDC 371.2—dc23
LC record available at https://lccn.loc.gov/2020044091
LC ebook record available at https://lccn.loc.gov/2020044092

∞™ The paper used in this publication meets the minimum requirements of American National Standard for Information Sciences—Permanence of Paper for Printed Library Materials, ANSI/NISO Z39.48-1992.

This book is dedicated to all the leaders who make a difference in the lives of students every day.

Contents

List of Figures and Tables

FIGURES

TABLES

Preface to *Preparing to Lead in a Digital Age*

Collegial conversations always seem to be recursive. A fellow educator poses a question to you. A hallway conversation ensues. A seed is planted. You find yourself thinking about the question often. You follow up with another conversation, or the topic becomes temporarily dormant—covered by a blanket of daily to-do's. Then the two of you find yourselves together at a professional conference. Your minds are focused on enhancing professional development. The to-do's are back on campus. The seed planted now finds fertile soil and begins to take root.

And so a question becomes the foundation for a book. The need is identified; chapter titles are drafted. Possible contributors discussed, added, and contacted.

Preparing to Lead in a Digital Age grew from our roots as K-12 educators who became teacher-leaders and teacher-educators. Our hallway conversation focused on texts to use to support educators and educational leaders in becoming knowledgeable practitioners using technology in pedagogically meaningful ways. We both felt the need for a book that provided a balance of theory and practice. We wanted a book that would resonate with future or current educational leaders in identifying real-world challenges and offering solutions.

THEMES WITHIN AND AMONG CHAPTERS

Voices of technology leaders speaking to collegial readers form the themes emerging from individual chapters and woven in a recursive pattern, serving to strengthen and connect the parts to the whole. We begin at the foundational beginning. Chapters 1 and 2 focus on making the transition to digital learning and the critical "why" of those steps. These initial chapters become touchstones to support teacher-leaders throughout their journey of becoming digital educators and leaders.

Chapters 3 and 4 introduce the tools of the technology trade. Tools firmly tethered to the principles of TPACK, SAMR, and student-centered learning. Beyond the belief of today's students needing to be engaged through a "look at the shiny" approach of technology tools in the classroom, these chapters focus again on the pedagogical practices supported by the tools.

Chapters 5 and 6 build upon the themes of student-centered learning while refining the lens to focus on supporting the specific, individual needs of these students. The principles of technology to support differentiated instruction are foundational in these chapters.

In Chapters 7, 8, and 9, the lens pulls back again, inviting the reader to consider how to engage in the evaluative process of sorting through the plethora of technology tools and resources available, the role of professional development and technology, and coaching others in the meaningful use of technology.

CHAPTER COMPASS

To guide the reader in their journey of preparing to lead in a digital age, a chapter compass may prove helpful. This compass leads the reader on a patterned path, a repeated structure. Each chapter begins with a real-world scenario, presented as an opportunity for the reader to step into the shoes of a fellow teacher-leader facing familiar challenges of teaching and leading in a digital age. The scenario is extended beyond a brief vignette, serving as a thread to connect foundational principles to real-world applications. The scenarios also offer the reader the opportunity to deeply engage in the type of decision-making all effective leaders employ. This intentionality as a digital leader is particularly emphasized in these scenarios.

Each chapter concludes with a series of "Reflect and Apply Activities" designed to support our goal of a text that promotes the growth of the digital leader. The reader is encouraged to engage in those activities to deepen their ability to apply theory in specific settings.

TO JOURNEY ALONE OR WITH TRUSTED COMPANIONS?

Our belief that collaboration in a community is at the heart of education, at the heart of who were as educators, should be abundantly evident by now. While there is no one right way to read and engage with this text, we encourage readers to read with a colleague, as part of a professional learning community, or with a small group of aspiring leaders. Some readers may find this text on the syllabus of a graduate course, so classmates become the collaborative community. However this book is read, we hope readers find it important, impactful, and enjoyable.

WITH GRATITUDE

The contributors whose expertise is shared in each chapter of the book are the voices of those practitioners living the foundational principles woven throughout the text. We are grateful for the individual and collective voices of these digital leaders, and the knowledge, expertise, and passion they bring to their profession.

Acknowledgment

Our most sincere thanks to Carlie Wall and the editorial staff for going above and beyond to make this book a success.

Chapter 1

Transition to Digital Learning

Avoiding "Panic-gogy"

Lin Carver and Lauren Pantoja

Lindsey Harris got up from her computer and stretched. She looked around her "home office" which was really a table in her dining room strewn with books, notepads, a calendar, pens and pencils, and of course, her computer. As she stared down at her computer screen, she thought about the Zoom lesson she had just finished. Six of her twenty-five students had joined the lesson. The attendance for the online lessons was abysmal, and the completion of the online assignments in her course even worse. She had tried everything she could think of to motivate and engage her students, mostly struggling learners, in this digital curriculum, but her efforts had only a little impact. The fact that student participation had increased even marginally was something to celebrate.

This was the fourth week of online distance learning that had been expeditiously implemented when schools across the state, across the country, and world really, closed to prevent the spread of the highly contagious virus, COVID-19. She was impressed with the curriculum her district had created to support learners in this time of crisis. Now, if she could just get her students to do the work. Lindsey sat back down and looked at the notepad with a list of parents she planned to call today in front of her. She looked at her cell phone and punched her first phone number into the keypad from her Google Voice account. She could hear the phone ringing multiple times and was just about to hang up when a male voice hoarsely responded with, "Hello." Lindsey sighed, relieved that someone answered and began, "Mr. Wilson, this is Jared's teacher, Ms. Harris."

INTRODUCTION

Leading in a digital learning environment can be a challenging experience! Technology has invaded education. Data indicated that as of 2016 public schools in the United States provided an average of one computer for every five students while spending $3 billion per year on digital content (Herold, 2016). In classrooms, tablets like Google's Chromebooks are becoming abundant because of their ease in management, inexpensive cost, and range of educational software. Math instruction is being enhanced through DreamBox, Zearn, and ST Math software. Language arts programs like No Red Ink, Achieve 3000, and Newsela are providing students with various ways to understand and process printed texts. Software such as Quizlet, Kahoot, and Plickers are becoming widely used to help educators manage their classrooms and assess student learning (Bernard, 2017).

However, technology is constantly changing and evolving as new programs, software, and apps are being developed daily. Consequently, educators need to repeatedly revise and update their skills. Spring 2020 made this reality abundantly evident as we were faced with unprecedented worldwide school closures due to governmental stay-at-home orders. But education was not the only sphere impacted. The staggering and widespread impacts of COVID-19 were evidenced by the abrupt curtailment of all markets, education, commerce, sporting events, banking, entertainment, community and religious meetings, and social interactions in virtually all regions of the world. Worldwide closures, raging viruses, high unemployment, and spiraling death tolls provide the basis for science fiction novels, not real life. Only a few short months after it first appeared, COVID-19 was classified by the World Health Organization as a pandemic because of individual's lack of immunity to the disease and its rapid spread across large regions of the earth (Kandola, 2020). Education had experienced intermittent disruptions due to natural disasters, but it had never experienced anything on the scale of the pandemic of 2020.

What is required of educational leaders as they prepare for the transition to or support of online or digitally enhanced learning? In what ways should educators support their staff as they attempt to reach and support their students? In what way does totally online instruction differ from the process of infusing technology into face-to-face instruction?

As educational leaders, it is important to understand the ramifications of mandated school closures on the educational system, the students it serves, and their families. By early March 2020, school closures had impacted 290 million children (McCarthy, 2020) and this number grew to 421 million students by mid-March (Tam & El-Azar, 2020). By the beginning of April that number had grown to 1,576,021,818 (91 percent) of learners from PK to upper secondary school worldwide. Around the world, education was disrupted for 91.3 percent learners from 188 countries (UNESCO, 2020). Many areas instituted stay-at-home orders which impacted about 94.5 percent of the U.S. population or about 306.3 million people (Secon & Woodward, 2020). *Education Week* reported that at least 123,000 U.S. public and private schools and 55.1 million students were impacted by these school closures. Some schools closed for weeks, while others remained closed for the remainder of the academic year (CRPE, 2000).

Because of mandated school closures, most schools shifted to some form of online learning (Goldstein, 2020). Because of this process, educational institutions were faced with a myriad of difficult decisions. Should educators stop instruction and simply continue education after the virus was under control? This was the hope should the pandemic be short-lived. Should districts distribute paper resources rather than focusing on digital resources? This would ensure that students without digital access were not deprived of educational content. Should all instruction be provided online? This solution came with a myriad of challenges—being certain all students had computers and internet access was the most basic.

Attempting to answer so many questions in such a short period of time resulted in "panic-gogy" (panic + pedagogy) (Kamenetz, 2020). Many districts had been attempting to integrate technology, but most districts were not prepared to present all instruction online. Leadership is the most important factor impacting a school's integration of technology. Schools that have made the most progress in integrating technology are the ones with energetic and committed leaders (National Center for Education Statistics, 2002).

Attempting to just move content from face-to-face classrooms into an online environment creates significant problems and challenges, even for the most energetic, committed leaders. But attempting to accomplish that move in the midst of a pandemic compounds those problems (Kamenetz, 2020).

HEALTH AND SAFETY CONCERNS

During this pandemic, students who were previously enrolled in local public K-12 schools faced many challenges. Districts had to understand the physical, social, and academic challenges their students were facing. In order to address the physical concerns, districts were closed in an attempt to safeguard the health of their students. The focus then shifted to meeting children's physical needs for food (Lake & Dusseault, 2020). Districts transitioned their free or reduced lunch programs so that children had food. Then they looked to virtual ways to establish social, support groups, and organize volunteers and employees to address students' physical, emotional, and social needs (Lake & Dusseault, 2020).

DIGITAL DIVIDE

Choosing the appropriate method for delivering instruction was the next area of concern. If instruction was to be provided, educators needed to decide if the materials should be treated as supplemental learning covering related topics of content previously covered, enrichment to expand on the current standards, review material on standards already covered, or whether it should be new curriculum. Then the institutions needed to decide if students should be required to complete the work to earn credit in their current course or if students were not required to complete the work to earn credit.

Challenges abound when attempting to move a district from face-to-face instruction to online instruction. About a third of the districts interviewed by *The New York Times* Editorial Board (2020) reported that they were attempting to distribute digital devices to their students who needed them. Students without internet access faced additional challenges because significantly fewer districts were providing mobile phones or Wi-Fi hotspots to students. Consequently, remote learning could have a disproportionately negative impact on low income and struggling learners (Goldstein, 2020) because not every family had computers or high-speed internet during this challenging time.

Shortages of digital devices resulted in the rationing of laptops, tablets, and mobile hotspots (Lake & Dusseault, 2020). New York City schools had only 25,000 devices available for its 300,000 students

(Wooley et al., 2020). The Hillsborough County School District in Florida only distributed one digital device per family. Anchorage public schools, on the other hand, distributed digital devices to older students rather than younger students (Lake & Dusseault, 2020). But just finding digital devices for students to use was not the only problem. Districts also needed to make sure that the devices could accomplish what the students needed them to do (Lloyd, 2020).

The issue of providing equitable instruction for all students was the next concern. Addressing the needs of students with learning disabilities became paramount. The U.S. Department of Education allowed for flexibility in complying with the federal disability laws during this emergency (Silva, 2020). This relaxation of the regulations actually created additional concerns. Without a precedent or guidebook, system leaders, educators, and parents tried to support students but were not sure of the best way to accomplish this for students with disabilities and other marginalized groups.

Minneapolis public schools addressed this issue by developing a distance learning plan that included providing guidance for accommodating Individualized Education Plans (IEPs), distributing assistive technology, and measuring the progress for students with disabilities during the COVID-19 pandemic. The plan also addressed the needs of other subgroups by outlining specific strategies for supporting English Language Learners, homeless students, American Indian families, and other vulnerable or marginalized groups (Lake & Dusseault, 2020).

Palm Beach County, Florida, is another example of a district creatively addressing all students' needs. Their plan included continuing services for migrant students and classes for English Language Learners. In addition, general education teachers would be responsible for accommodating students with disabilities, but special education teachers' role would expand to include supporting both students and families. IEP meetings would continue through phone or digital platforms because of social distancing measures (Lake & Dusseault, 2020).

Districts discovered that in some cases students' accommodations could be provided in the online classroom platform through speech-to-text, highlighting capability, and flexible scheduling. Students could continue to receive small group and one-on-one support with a teacher via audio and video conferencing and collaboration. Counselors, behavior specialists, social workers, and all student services team members were available to both students and parents (Musselwhite, 2020).

MATCHING METHOD TO STUDENT NEEDS

Challenges presented by a lack of digital devices were only one concern. Educational leaders scrambled to construct quality online programs to support students during this challenging time. However, research with remote learning suggested that moving children to an online learning environment presented significantly different challenges than doing so with adults (Goldstein, 2020). Younger children require a lot of supervision by an adult, teachers do not always have expertise in creating online lessons, students with learning needs may struggle with self-discipline, and many students may not be comfortable speaking on the telephone with teachers who are calling to support them (Goldstein, 2020).

Learners and their families were faced with having to determine the learning method that worked most effectively for them. Those students who had access to a computer with internet connection could explore the options provided by their local district or could chose to enroll in a different virtual school setting. Florida was able to quickly transition to online learning in part because it is home to the Florida Virtual School which has been in existence for twenty years with an enrollment of 200,000 students from many different states and from overseas (Kamenetz, 2020). During this crisis, Florida Virtual School increased its capacity so that it would be able to serve 2.7 million students during the COVID-19 school closures; this was ten times more students than they had served the previous year. During the pandemic Florida Virtual School provided 100 free courses for K–12 students from general education courses to advanced placement (Dailey, 2020). Some students chose to move to a virtual school setting, but because learning is a social process, others wanted to remain with their classmates and teachers in their zoned district.

DECISIONS

Even if a district made the decision to place instruction online and the student chose to stay with the district curriculum, there were additional challenges. They also needed to consider the coherence of instruction. They needed to determine how what they provided online built on what they had been doing in the classroom. Educators were inundated with suggestions for digital materials they could use. But the digital materials available did not necessarily constitute sets of lessons that built or scaffolded on one another. They were not necessarily tied to academic standards for each subject and each grade level (Rand, 2020). During this crisis districts developed learning plans to meet the needs of their students. These learning plans often required parents, who were already overwhelmed with balancing working from home, meeting financial obligations because of unemployment challenges, providing extensive childcare, and monitoring and tracking multiple children's academic progress, to provide the instructional support their students needed. During this pandemic project-based learning assignments were developed for all students in the Houston Independent School District. The district plan included teachers' check in calls, but the plan depended heavily on student initiative and parental support for establishing and maintaining the daily academic routine (Lake & Dusseault, 2020).

When a district decided to move to online instruction, the first question they needed to answer was what did digital learning mean to them? What components should it include? Districts might decide to include prepared content, blended learning, flipped learning, personalized learning, or other strategies that use digital tools in varying degrees (Davis, 2020). No matter what components the district decided to include, they first needed to prepare the digital devices. This required a significant time investment to ensure that each device had the appropriate operating systems and software programs. Then the districts needed to examine the free or paid learning management system (LMS) currently being used. Many districts are using Canvas, Blackboard, or Google Classroom for a small portion of their instruction, but each system comes with its own unique challenges. Educators needed to consider if the current LMS could support the extra demands that would be placed on the system or would additional licenses need to be purchased to support the increased demand.

Preparing to learn securely and safely with students is a concern. Technology specialists had to determine the appropriate security settings for each program so that students were not exposed to possible negative influences online. But just as educators determined the appropriate settings, companies were changing their settings in an attempt to solve the same problem. The software companies made changes, and then technology specialists needed to share the updated information with instructors (Lake, 2020). One example is the popular videoconferencing tool Zoom. The company reported that in December of 2019, they had ten million users; by March of 2020, with people working from home and school closures due to the pandemic, 200 million people were using the app on a daily basis (Bond, 2020). This hasty and massive movement to video conferencing opened the door to security issues, and what became widely known as "Zoom bombing" began to take place. On March 30, 2020, the Federal Bureau of Investigation's (FBI) Boston office reported that they had received "multiple reports of conferences being interrupted by pornographic and/or hate images and threatening language" (Setera, 2020, para. 1). The Zoom company quickly reacted by placing a focus on repairing security and privacy issues which included changing settings for schools and universities to default to more privacy and publishing a guide on how to protect meetings (Lake, 2020).

Synchronous instruction did not seem to be the choice of most districts. Instead many are using "asynchronous" or "hybrid" remote learning through the use of instructional videos or daily assignments with feedback (Lake, 2020). Many districts began the distance learning experience by providing enrichment materials, but as the length of time in distance learning grew, they moved from enrichment to instruction. For example, when Governor J. B. Pritzker of Illinois extended school closures through the end of April, he ordered school districts to transition from enrichment to remote learning days (Lake & Dusseault, 2020).

PROFESSIONAL LEARNING

Supporting teachers during the transition from face-to-face to online instruction was a significant concern so as not to end up in a "panicgogy" where anything goes. Educators solved this challenge in a variety of ways. Two Utah Valley school districts prepared to move instruction online by having digital coaches set up simultaneous trainings in ten different locations throughout the district. Training included information on the learning platform, methods of assessment, video-recording options, and the software programs available. Small teams from each school went back to their own school to train other teachers based on the training they had just received. Although the process allowed for rapid sharing of information, the districts found that the coaches' stress level increased because they were trying to answer questions about programs and methods with which they were just becoming familiar (Lloyd, 2020). Other districts chose to make use of professional development available online. For example, Florida Virtual School partnered with districts to provide professional development for teachers during the move to emergency online learning (Kamenetz, 2020).

As these teachers and coaches discovered, with any ed-tech tools, it is important to have a thorough knowledge and understanding of the tools so that instructors are able to troubleshoot for their students and themselves. The ever-expanding variety of apps and platforms makes it difficult to identify the tools that most effectively support student learning. The rapid transition to online learning because of the pandemic did not allow time for this knowledge building process (Gannon, 2019).

An important consideration was whether educators would be using prepared digital resources or whether they would be responsible for preparing their own digital content. If instructors were using software that the district had already purchased, such as iReady or Achieve 3000, these teachers needed training to familiarize themselves on how to operate, use, and track students' progress in the specific program. Using either free or paid versions of resources such as EngageNY, LearnZillion, and Open Up resources would help teachers to more effectively align instruction to the state standards. Teachers could begin with these options and then determine the digital resources to support the curriculum (Rand, 2020).

If the district chose to have the teachers create the content, there were significantly more concerns. A thoughtful integration of technology which enables students to engage with their peers and enhance the learning experience (Davis, 2020) is the goal, but whether the speed of this transition during this "panic-gogy" enabled this is another issue. Shortly before the beginning of the pandemic, Schoology conducted a study called "The State of Digital Learning." The survey of 16,906 teachers and administrators, with nearly 97 percent of these from the United States, provided information about the state of digital integration in education. The majority of K-12 teachers and administrators who completed the survey agreed that technology positively impacted student growth and achievement. They also observed that online instruction can enhance learning experiences, save teachers time, enable instructors to better tailor learning to student needs, aid in tracking student progress, and provide transparency in the learning process (Davis, 2020). In teacher-created distance learning during this unprecedented time, instructors needed training on the additional technological resources that can be used.

Video conferencing platforms such as Zoom, Go to Meeting, Teams, and WebEx are being used to provide support and instruction to teachers as they transition to online instruction. These tools allow for social distancing while providing visual contact and content sharing between participants thus providing another venue for preparing teachers. Digital websites such as Boclips has made videos available to teachers which can be used to align instruction with standards. This program also provides resources for helping teachers learn how to incorporate videos into their lessons. YouTube, the go to source for many of us, also provided short videos which can be used to familiarize teachers with many additional resources. However, having time to explore and develop an understanding of tools during this crisis is certainly a luxury.

Some districts make the decision to treat the online instruction occurring during this pandemic as a portion of the student's grade. This decision raises concerns about how assessment will be conducted. Some districts have chosen to use software such as Proctorio, a Google Chrome extension that monitors students taking exams online, in an attempt to create a more secure environment for assessment.

PROVIDING ONLINE INSTRUCTION

Putting a course online requires more than just taking the content used in the face-to-face setting and posting it on a digital platform. In a digital environment, the lack of gestures, vocal inflections, stress, and facial expressions can cause information to be perceived in a totally different light than intended. Consequently, it is imperative for the instructor to carefully consider the tone of written comments and text. One widely used strategy for written feedback is the "sandwich" approach which is particularly effective in instruction whether online or face-to-face. The first layer of feedback in the sandwich approach is a positive comment about something the student did well. The middle comment is constructive; it focuses on a critical analysis of the content of the assignment and is aligned to the specifications of the assignment and/or the rubric. The instructor might include suggestions or a direction for improving the student's work. The final layer of feedback in the sandwich approach is similar to the top layer in that it incorporates something positive about the assignment, but it also includes encouragement and invites the student to use the information moving forward for rethinking or restructuring their work (Kulmala, 2011). This approach allows for constructive feedback, which is essential for students' cognitive growth, but provides a formula for providing the feedback in an encouraging manner that is less likely to be misinterpreted.

However, it is still much easier to guide learners to a more skillful or thorough response in person than it is to accomplish the same feat by providing written feedback where even carefully phrased comments may be perceived as harsh or punitive. Creating engaging discussions, constructing blogging forums, and curating applicable resources to accompany online course content, all require a significant time investment. Students' attitude toward online activities is another important consideration. Students reported that they felt more engaged and received more immediate feedback in face-to-face discussion than in online discussion. They strongly preferred to discuss course content with peers in the classroom rather than online (Kemp & Grieve, 2014). It is evident that online course construction requires a totally different process than just compiling textbook-based lecture notes and discussion questions from your face-to-face class (Gannon, 2019). All of these online course construction skills are competencies which we have not had the time to thoroughly develop during this mass transition to online learning.

As instructors consider their digital courses, an important first consideration is how to present the content. Videos are an effective way to supplement instruction because they provide both visual and auditory support to further clarify the content. However, instructors should not try to convert the entire lecture into a video. Videos should be limited to maximum of thirty minutes because of learners' limited attention spans and their inability to remember too much content at once. A series of short videos broken into sections is a much better choice (Gerwin, 2020). Short videos make the content more memorable and are easier for students to replay if they become confused or they want to review the information.

However, creating a video takes a long time even when using tools with which you are familiar. Creating videos typically requires three times as much work as a traditional lecture (Gannon, 2019). Another option that instructors may want to explore would be cutting portions of already created videos to support the instructional content (Gannon, 2019). Video-sharing programs, like EdPuzzle, offer instructors several strategies for monitoring and enhancing student learning while they are viewing videos. Once a video is selected from a variety of online resources in EdPuzzle, the instructor can crop it, provide voiceover, or insert notes. Formative assessments can be added in the form of multiple-choice, true or false, or open-ended questions at various points in the video (Mischel, 2018). No matter how the video content is presented within the online course, it is important to make sure to include captioning or transcripts to comply with the Americans with Disabilities Act (Gannon, 2019).

In all instruction, both in the face-to-face and online classroom, the instructor does not need to be the "sage on the stage." This is especially important in the online classroom. Instructors need to increase student engagement by encouraging student participation through feedback and peer discussions. Digital tools that afford students substantive ways of interacting with peers and the instructor while engaging deeply with the course materials or applications are particularly important in online learning. Tools such as Hypothes.is, a web annotation tool, or Padlet, which enables collaborative digit spaces, can engage learners while enhancing student discussions. Instructors tend to be limited by the features within their LMS or those that can be used in conjunction with the LMS. Many LMS include blog space features; however, if the district's LMS does not have one, a tool like WordPress blog could be used.

When constructing an online course, consider the integration of digital tools within the online content. Choose an appropriate digital tool to accomplish a specific instructional learning goal rather than just identifying free or trendy tools. An effective digital tool should provide a match between the specific content, learning goals, and learners. The appropriate integration of all of these features require both time and a well-developed plan which is what makes this current transition to online learning so difficult (Gannon, 2019).

As with all instruction, it is important for teachers to connect with students often to enhance learning, to identify students who are struggling, and to provide any needed support. Research has found that during the transition to online learning almost every student experiences some type of "performance penalty." This can become evidenced through lower grades than they earned previously, difficulty in completing assignments on time, or even failure to complete the required assignments or courses. Learners who are struggling with the transition to online learning because of social or academic challenges are particularly vulnerable to the performance penalty (Hart et al., 2017).

AVAILABLE RESOURCES

During the pandemic, many digital resources were offered for free, with more companies adding additional options each day. How long each of these would remain free was still unknown, but the free options were a wonderful way for instructors to experiment with features to help their students. Even if these resources change from a free to a paid status, they would be valuable resources to consider incorporating into online instruction.

Core content instruction can be provided through such programs as Achieve 3000 which offered free access to resources for differentiating literacy instruction either in a print or digital format during the pandemic. "Achieve 3000 Literacy at Home" includes the different levels of non-fiction science, social studies, and current events articles. "Actively Learn," a resource for 6–12th graders, incorporates contemporary and classic literature for science, social studies, and English Language Arts. For those learners who do not have access to internet connection, "Literacy Printable Packets" contain twenty articles with questions.

During the pandemic various resources have been made available. For example, the American Museum of Natural History, Arizona State University, and Amplify are providing free lessons on various topics from anthropology to zoology, virtual field trips, videos, puzzles, photos, and maps. English Language Learners or those learning a foreign language can be supported through the digital program Babbel which is currently offering three months of free language learning in any of the languages the program includes. Teachers and students can work collaboratively writing books through programs like Book Creator which is offering a free 90-day upgrade to its premium service. These cultural and creative experiences provide a glimpse into the expanse of online resources available.

CONCLUSION

As we have discussed, there are many issues to consider when creating an effective distance learning plan. Moving from face-to-face to online instruction can be a difficult process. Districts first need to assess the hardware and software resources available for distance learning. Then the district will need to determine what families have available and procure what is needed to provide equitable access to all students. Districts need to consider that the longer they are providing instruction online, the greater the gaps will become that need to be filled. Identifying the curriculum and providing training for faculty, staff, and families is the next step. Then educators will need to develop policies for hardware distribution and make sure that technology professionals are available to continue supporting the process (Schaffhauser, 2020).

During this time of crisis, many learners are experiencing online learning for the first time. An online course can provide a powerful learning experience for helping learners become deeply engaged with the content. But this engagement is not accomplished by chance. It is accomplished when instructors and learners are present in the course and interacting with each other. The instructor presence might be the single most important ingredient in making the online learning meaningful. Research has determined that instructor presence needs to incorporate both social and cognitive features. In the absence of either the social or cognitive presence, online courses are no different from having a group of passive recipients crammed into an impersonal lecture hall. If this is the experience our learners receive during this pandemic, they may as well just view videos. As districts, technology specialists, and instructors work together we will be able to refine, expand, and improve on the instruction our students are receiving online.

The transition from face-to-face instruction to online instruction took us all by surprise. Although this was a difficult time, businesses, community members, educational leaders, and teachers across the United States came together to maintain as much normalcy as possible and quickly provided students with an online educational program. Technology even with its many challenges and difficulties has invaded and taken over education. There is no manual to support the transition or guidebook for providing the best possible transition (Lloyd, 2020). As teachers refine their skills in the area of distance education, the possibilities are becoming more evident. What we have learned is that flexibility and patience were necessary, especially in the beginning of the transition to online learning, and that both students and teachers needed to give themselves time and permission to work through issues and just figure it all out (Merrill, 2020). During this time of social distancing, we have also learned so much about the possibilities and the various options available for distance learning. Online learning does not look the same in every setting.

Whether technology and online learning has forever changed education or whether it has only introduced more options remains to be seen. For right now, technology is providing the social connections that we are craving. It is also providing a venue for continuing student learning, but what the future holds for educational technology and the role it will play in education remains to be seen.

REFLECT AND APPLY ACTIVITIES

1.1 Reflect on the impact COVID-19 had on your personal and professional life. What did you learn about providing digital learning from this experience? Using scholarly sources identify some processes you would refine if you were to make the transition to totally online learning

1.2 Based on the information in this chapter, your personal experience, and other scholarly resources, what are some of the steps the educational system can take to reduce the impact of the digital divide on our students with economic or academic challenges? Additionally, how can digital resources be used to address equity for all students?

REFERENCES

Bernard, Z. (2017, December 27). Here's how technology is shaping the future of education. *Business Insider.* https://www.businessinsider.com/how-technology-is-shaping-the-future-of-education-2017-12.

Bond, S. (2020, April 3). A must for millions, Zoom has a dark side—and an FBI warning. *NPR-WUSF Public Media.* https://www.npr.org/2020/04/03/826129520/a-must-for-millions-zoom-has-a-dark-side-and-an-fbi-warning.

Center on Reinventing Public Education (CRPE). (2020). *District Responses to COVID-19 School Closures.* https://www.crpe.org/content/covid-19-school-closures.

Dailey, R. (2020, April 1). Florida Virtual School beefing up capacity to serve 2.7 million students amid COVID-19 closures. *WFSU News.* https://news.wfsu.org/post/florida-virtual-school-beefing-capacity-serve-27-million-students-amid-covid-19-closures.

Davis, L. (2020, February 6). Digital learning: What to know in 2020. *Schoology Exchange.* https://www.schoology.com/blog/digital-learning.

Gannon, K. (2019, March 25). 4 lessons from moving a face-to-face course online. *ChronicleVitae.* https://chroniclevitae.com/news/2176-4-lessons-fro m-moving-a-face-to-face-course-online.

Goldstein, D. (2020, March 17). Coronavirus is shutting schools. Is America ready for virtual learning? *The New York Times.* https://www.nytimes.com/2 020/03/13/us/virtual-learning-challenges.html.

Hart, C., Friedman, E., & Hill, M. (2017). Online course-taking and student outcomes in California community colleges. *Education Finance and Policy, 13*(1). https://www.mitpressjournals.org/doi/abs/10.1162/edfp_a_00218.

Herold, B. (2016, February 5). Technology in education: An overview. *Education Week.* https://www.edweek.org/ew/issues/technology-in-education/ index.html.

Kamenetz, A. (2020, March 19). Panic-gogy: Teaching online classes during the coronavirus pandemic. *NPR.* https://www.npr.org/2020/03/19/817885991/ panic-gogy-teaching-online-classes-during-the-coronavirus-pandemic.

Kamenetz, A. (2020, March 26). The biggest distance-learning experiment in history: Week one. *Mind Shift* [Audio podcast]. https://www.kqed.org/mind shift/55650/the-biggest-distance-learning-experiment-in-history-week-one.

Kandola, A. (2020, March 17). Coronavirus cause: Origin and how it spreads. *Medial News Today.* https://www.medicalnewstoday.com/articles/coronavi rus-causes.

Kemp, N., & Grieve, R. (2014, November 12). Face-to-face or face-to-screen? Undergraduates' opinions and test performance in classrooms vs. online learning. *Frontiers in Psychology, 5.* https://www.ncbi.nlm.nih.gov/pmc/ar ticles/PMC4228829/.

Kulmala, D. (2011, April 14). To increase learner achievement serve feedback sandwiches. *Faculty Focus.* https://www.facultyfocus.com/articles/teaching -and-learning/to-increase-learner-achievement-serve-feedback-sandwiches/.

Lake, R. (2020, March 28). The latest from a nationwide survey: Districts continue to struggle toward online learning. *The Lens.* https://www.crpe.org /thelens/latest-nationwide-survey-districts-continue-struggle-toward-online -learning.

Lake, R., & Dusseault, B. (2020, April 3). School systems make a slow transition from the classroom to the cloud. *The Lens.* https://www.crpe.org/ thelens/school-systems-make-slow-transition-classroom-cloud.

Lloyd, J. (2020, April 14). Utah Valley school districts proud of technology successes after COVID-19 forces dramatic changes. *Daily Herald.* https:// www.heraldextra.com/news/local/education/precollegiate/utah-valley-schoo l-districts-proud-of-technology-successes-after-covid-19-forced-dramatic -changes/article_a968c2d5-af4b-5e6b-b961-a38cf562632a.html.

McCarthy, K. (2020, March 6). The global impact of coronavirus on education. *ABC News.* https://abcnews.go.com/International/global-impact-coronavirus -education/story?id=69411738.

Merrill, S. (2020, March 19). Teaching through a pandemic: A mindset for this moment. *Edutopia*. https://www.edutopia.org/article/teaching-through-pandemic-mindset-moment?gclid=Cj0KCQjw-Mr0BRDyARIsAKEFbecxyj tm6-ISD3j_WWEk_y5O13999EIHnRO2yZc_nd81i8d6dJrAE74aAvS7E ALw_wcB.

Mischel, L. (2018, May 7). Watch and learn? Using Edpuzzle to enhance the use of online videos. *Management Teaching Review, 4*(3), 283–289. https:// journals.sagepub.com/doi/10.1177/2379298118773418.

Musselwhite, M. (2020, March 22). *Students with Disabilities FAQ*. [Video]. https://www.youtube.com/watch?v=dyGBas2jsAo.

National Center for Education Statistics. (2002). *Technology in Schools*. https ://nces.ed.gov/pubs2003/tech_schools/chapter7.asp.

New York Time Editorial Board. (2020, April 6). The teachers union ate my homework. *Wall Street Journal*. https://www.wsj.com/articles/the-teachers -union-ate-my-homework 11586214731.

Rand. (2020, April 2). Schools pivot online in wake of COVID-19: Q & A with Rand experts. *Rand Blog*. https://www.rand.org/blog/2020/04/schools-pivot -online-in-wake-of-covid-19-qampa-with.html.

Schaffhauser, D. (2020, April 4). 8 Steps for developing a robust plan for distance learning. *THE Journal*. https://thejournal.com/Articles/2020/04/23 /8-Steps-for-Developing-a-Robust-Plan-for-Distance-Learning.aspx?s=the _nu_290420&oly_enc_id=6101J6588889G0K&Page=1.

Secon, H., & Woodward, A. (2020, April 7). About 95% of Americans have been ordered to stay at home. *Business Insider*. https://www.businessinsider .com/us-map-stay-at-home-orders-lockdowns-2020-3.

Setera, K. (2020, March 30). FBI warns of teleconferencing and online class-room hijacking during COVID-19 pandemic. *FBI, Boston*. https://www.fbi .gov/contact-us/field-offices/boston/news/press-releases/fbi-warns-of-telec onferencing-and-online-classroom-hijacking-during-covid-19-pandemic.

Silva, E. (2020, March 31). What school closure means for students with disabilities. *New America*. https://www.newamerica.org/education-policy/e dcentral/what-school-closures-mean-students-disabilities/.

Tam, G., & El-Azar, D. (2020, March 13). 3 Ways the coronavirus pandemic could reshape education. *World Economic Forum*. https://www.weforum. org/agenda/2020/03/3-ways-coronavirus-is-reshaping-education-and-what-changes-might-be-here-to-stay/.

UNESCO. (2020, April 4). *COVID-19 Educational Disruption and Response*. Author. https://en.unesco.org/covid19/educationresponse.

Wooley, S., Sattiraju, N., & Mortiz, S. (2020, March 26). U. S. schools trying to teach online highlight a digital divide. *Bloomberg*. https://www.bloomber g.com/news/articles/2020-03-26/COVID-19-school-closures-reveal-dispari ty-in-access-to-internet.

Chapter 2

Foundations for Technology Integration

Holly Atkins

At a district-wide principals' meeting, Latoya Williamson and her peers received their marching orders—improve the quality of technology use at your site. As Latoya drove home, she considered her next steps. Training. Yes, there will need to be additional training for her faculty on the effective use of technology. Develop a plan. Yes, the training needs to be part of a broader school-wide strategic plan. Where are we going? How do we get there? And most importantly, what will "there" look like? Latoya pondered these issues. While district leaders had identified (and rightly so) a pervasive issue—lack of effective use of technology the vision of what school-wide meaningful use of technology would look like had been left to the individual principals.

As an academic leader, Latoya wondered how her technology use measured up. What exactly did the district view as the appropriate level of technology integration? Did her usage reflect the "appropriate level" she wondered? Latoya decided she was fairly tech-savvy. Her smartphone was always with her. She was constantly juggling multiple forms of communication from texts to emails, to phone calls. She completed most of her administrative tasks through technology. So, technology was used in many facets of her job.

But as she thought more about instruction, she wondered to what extent she really used technology as an instructional tool. She did PowerPoint presentations, of course. And, yes, she was pretty good at adding images, limiting the text on her slides, etc. Personally, she used social media to some extent. She connected with friends and family via Facebook and Instagram. She had a Twitter account, but she rarely accessed it. Were those really instructional tools, Latoya wondered? Latoya understood the need for standards to form the foundation for curriculum development. But what were the standards that existed to help build a foundation for effective technology integration, she wondered?

STANDARDS

"Technology is supporting more of the full experience of learning, rather than just being relegated to supporting math drills, reading instruction practices and the like," stated Karen Cator, president and CEO of edtech nonprofit Digital Promise (Goset, 2020, para. 4). Cator's words serve as a call or challenge for educators to explore and apply the ever-expanding ways technology can support meaningful student learning beyond the mastery of basic factual information. Enter technology standards.

Standards are certainly a familiar concept to educators since they identify what students need to know and do in each grade level and in each academic area. In this same spirit of identifying specific learning goals, the International Society for Technology in Education (ISTE) developed the ISTE Standards as frameworks for digital age learning. ISTE Standards have been developed for students, educators, education leaders, and coaches, as well as computer science educators and computational thinking competencies.

First developed in 1998 and titled the National Educational Technology Standards (NETS), the initial focus was solely on students' technology skills. Standards for educators, education leaders, coaches, and for computational thinking (computer science courses) were developed later. While these standards provided the foundational principles, the standards have undergone frequent revisions in response to the ever-expanding uses of technology in education with an awareness that effective technology use must go beyond "by students" to "in education." The United States Department of Education Office of Educational Technology advocates for leaders to craft a vision for the use of technology by bringing "all stakeholder groups to the table, including students, educators, families, technology professionals, community groups, cultural institutions, and other interested parties" (Office of Educational Technology, 2020, p. 87). Expanding technology standards beyond the students to include many of those stakeholders helps to ensure that technology to support learning has both breadth and depth and is supported by knowledgeable practitioners (Garcia, 2014; Hirsh-Pasek et al., 2015; Purcell et al., 2013).

The ISTE Standards currently have been developed for students, teachers, coaches, and educational leaders and are clustered around foundational principles. For students these seven principles include Empowered Learner, Digital Citizen, Knowledge Constructor, Innovative Designer, Computational Thinking, Creative Communicator, and Global Collaborator. The seven principles are identified for teachers include Learner, Leader, Citizen, Collaborator, Designer, Facilitator and Analyst. For coaches there are again seven principles that are Change Agent, Connected Learner, Collaborator, Learning Designer, Professional Learning Facilitator, Data-Driven Decision-Maker, and Digital Citizen Advocate. The standards for educational leaders are built on five foundational principles: Equity and Citizenship Advocate, Visionary Planner, Empowering Leader, Systems Designer, and Connected Learner. Even though each group has its own ISTE Standards, there is overlap in many of the components.

WHAT DOES EFFECTIVE USE OF TECHNOLOGY *LOOK* LIKE?

Latoya understood that crafting a vision based on foundational standards for each member of her school community was an important first step. She also understood that as an instructional leader, she needed to empower her teachers with tools for them to determine what specifically effective use of technology can and should look like in their classrooms. Engaging teachers in reflecting on their practice and their use of technology is an important first step. Latoya can begin this process by developing a survey to gather data to determine what teachers perceive to be the school strengths and areas for growth in the integration of technology into instruction. If teachers are not aware of additional ways that technology can be integrated into instruction to support student learning, it will be difficult for them to further their technology integration. So, Latoya needs to understand what is currently being done so that teachers can be exposed to, explore, and incorporate additional digital possibilities.

Markers, chart paper, whiteboards, smartboards, tablets are all important components in a teacher's toolbox. As this toolbox continues to expand and develop, it enables teacher to embrace both old and new tools as well as high- and low-tech tools. Like the master carpenter or artist, the expert teacher understands how to select the best tool for each task. This focus on the "how" and "why" of technology usage reflects a move away from the emphasis on the "what tool" of technology.

Models such as SAMR and TPACK, as well as ISTE Standards, support teachers in developing a lens and framework to evaluate and reflect upon the meaningful use of technology. It is important to note that while SAMR, TPACK, the 4 Cs and the ISTE Standards provide a broad, guiding perspective on technology use, it is critical for educators to always focus on individual student's needs. With technology use, as with all instruction, one size does not fit all, and neither is the impact of technology effectively measured through a standardized lens or assessment. The need for differentiated instruction is informed and supported through effective, student-centered use and creation with technology.

SAMR

Referred to as a model, framework, or lens, SAMR is a tool to help in designing effective digital learning experiences (Schrock, 2019). Developed by Ruben R. Puentedura, the SAMR model was envisioned as a tool for categorizing classroom technology integration (2013) (see Figure 2.1). While often represented as a hierarchical ladder, it is more than that. The SAMR model should be used as a way to reflect on the entirety of technology use within the classroom.

The substitution level provides the foundation for technology usage, just as the Remembering level in Bloom's revised taxonomy of learning (Anderson & Krathwohl, 2001) provides the foundation for all other levels of cognition within the learning framework. Without the Remembering level all other thinking processes would not occur. The four domains of the SAMR model represent the totality of technology usage. It is vital to understand the impact of the specific tool on meeting the needs of the learner. When determining the appropriate SAMR

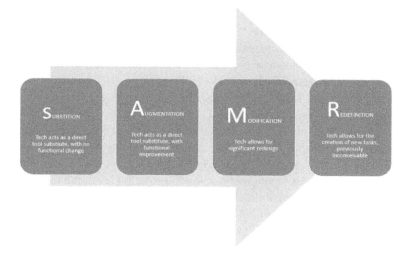

Figure 2.1 SAMR Model.

level at which the tool should be used, it is important to consider the impact of the TASK and the choice of the TOOL which when both are combined result in increased LEARNING.

Substitution

Substitution is the first level of the SAMR model. At this level technology is used as a direct substitution tool with no functional change. For the Substitution level, Puentedura's question of what is gained by replacing the older method with the new technology should be considered. If there is no gain, there is no point in using the technology.

At the Substitution level, traditional tools such as paper and pencil are replaced by a technology tool such as Microsoft Word or Google Docs. This level of technology usage is evidenced when a teacher displays a web-based version of a poem to use in a whole-class reading instead of providing students with paper copies of the poem. The digital version of the poem has the same function as the hard copy would have had.

Asking the reflective questions about why the technology tool is used and how it has impacted student learning can be especially important at this level. The teacher will need to decide what advantages there are to using a digital copy as compared to simply providing the hard copy? Perhaps by using a digital copy, students are able to access their own copy of the document on tablets or smartphones. This could simply be a financial decision motivated by limitation the school has placed on the number of paper copies the teacher is allowed to make. Rather than requiring students to share copies, they can be provided with their own personal copy from which to read.

However, the teacher might also be considering the needs of her learners with visual difficulties. Using a digital copy, students with visual impairments will be able to change the text font size, change from black on white to white on black text, or change the background to make the font easier to read. While the initial task and use of technology may appear to simply be at the Substitution level, the teacher's knowledge of the possibilities the tool provides and the understanding of students' needs result in differentiate instruction which helps to eliminate potential barriers to the students' learning. Both a whole class and individual student perspective is needed to fully reflect on the use of technology at the appropriate level. When used with intentionality as described earlier, what may first appear as the Substitution level can actually be used at the Augmentation level.

Augmentation

Augmentation is the next level where technology acts as a direct substitute with functional improvement. Sometimes what appears to be Substitution is actually Augmentation. With the above example of the poem for the class read aloud, when a digital copy of the poem is used students can also use the text-to-speech function or the translation function which are available on the digital device that would not be available with the print copy. Support for students with visual, reading, or language challenges could not have been provided with the printed copy of the poem. These functions move the use of the digital resource to the Augmentation level.

There are two questions to be considered when determining if a digital tool is being used at the Augmentation level. The teacher will want to consider if an improvement has been added to the task that could not be accomplished with the older method and how the features of the digital tool contribute or enhance the instructional design.

At the Augmentation level, technology still substitutes for the traditional tools; however, what is different is that there are enhancements that result in an improved learning experience. A basic web-based version of the poem would be at the Substitution level. A use of extensions and apps to change the appearance or presentation would be at the Augmentation level. Similarly, a web-based version that contains links to additional images of the setting or information about the historical background would be an example of using technology at the Augmentation level. Moving from the Substitution to the Augmentation level we begin to see how the learning experience is enhanced through the use of technology.

Modification

Modification is the next level where the use of technology allows for a significant redesign of the learning task. There are three questions to be considered when determining if a tool is being used at the Modification level. Teachers should consider how the original task is being modified, whether the modification depends on the new technology, and how the modification contributes to the design.

In the Modification level, the task and the resulting learning experience move beyond enhancement to transformation. The learning task is no longer only replaced by the use of technology; it takes on aspects that significantly enrich the task. Collaborative experiences within the digital environment are often evident in learning tasks at the Modification and Redefinition. An example of a task at the Modification level would occur when students use Google Docs to read and collaboratively annotate the whole class poem and then comment on each other's annotations. At this level students are working together on a task that would not be possible without the technology.

Redefinition

Redefinition is the final SAMR level. At this level the use of technology allows for the creation of a new task that would not be possible without the technology. There are four questions to be considered when determining if a tool is being used at the Redefinition level. Teachers will need to consider: What is the new task? Is any portion of the original task retained? How is the new task being made possible by the new technology? How does the technology contribute to the design?

The transformation of learning tasks is at a level where they would be impossible without the use of technology. Using the class poem example, if the whole class poem reading and annotating moved beyond the present class and connects the learners with other classes in other states or countries to compare how geographical and cultural influences impact its meaning, the activity has moved to the Redefinition level.

IT'S NOT THE TOOL; IT'S THE TEACHER

While SAMR offers an important tool for engaging educators in a conversation about what the effective use of technology looks like, many in the technology community have warned about the misuse of the SAMR tool (Anderson, 2015; Hamilton et al., 2016; France, 2018). Viewing SAMR as a ladder to climb to reach the pinnacle of Redefinition only results in pitting one teacher against another while moving the emphasis to the specific technology tool used rather than focusing on student learning. Using technology at the Redefinition level is not inherently better than using it at any other level.

Tech newbies and those already resistant to integrating technology into their classrooms view aiming for the Redefinition level as one more insurmountable obstacle to using technology to enhance instruction. The refrain Latoya and other educational leaders need to repeat is, "It's not the tool; it's the teacher." It is important to be mindful of focusing on technology as a tool to support teacher-designed learning experiences that meet their students' needs. Teachers need to recognize the value of Mark Anderson's words that "like any tool, technology is only as good as the person using it" (Anderson, 2015, para. 2). Like the master carpenter, the experienced educator knows how to reach into their toolbox and select the best tool for the learning task to address their students' needs. Technology helps to expand the possibilities in that toolbox.

Effective leaders understand the need to support their teachers with meaningful professional development that values where each teacher is and provides support for creating transformative learning experiences.

TPACK (TECHNOLOGY, PEDAGOGY, AND CONTENT KNOWLEDGE)

Effective, meaningful use of technology in the classroom is a complex endeavor involving the interplay between various forms of knowledge within an environment that greatly impacts the interaction. Koehler

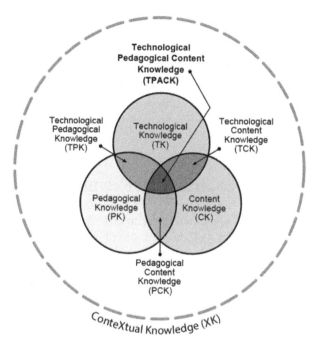

Figure 2.2   Revised Version of the TPACK image. © Punya Mishra, 2018. Reproduced with permission.

and Mishra (2009) offer the TPACK framework as a way to represent three primary forms of knowledge represented by overlapping knowledge: Content—knowledge of the subject matter being studied, Pedagogy—knowledge of teaching best practices to make learning happen, and Technology—knowing of when and how the use of technology improves completion of a task. Figure 2.2 illustrates each area of knowledge with a circle. The three circles are placed next to each other so that each overlaps with a small portion of the other. While each of the three circles of knowledge intersects with one another in various combinations, the center where all three of the adjacent knowledge circles intersect is the sweet spot in which Technological Pedagogical Content Knowledge occurs.

Koehler and Mishra's (2009) framework is built upon the foundational belief of effective learning for students resulting from the classroom teacher's deep understanding of their subject area combined with the knowledge of instructional practices that support student learning.

Teachers who have a breadth and depth of knowledge of the technology tools available are able to then make sound decisions as to how to match the tool with the content and the learning strategy. As an instructional leader, Latoya's ultimate goal is for meaningful student learning to happen throughout her school. She can use the TPACK model as a means of shifting the focus from the tool to how the teachers are using their expertise in content, pedagogy, and technology to increase student achievement.

DIGITAL CITIZENSHIP

A discussion of the foundational principles underscoring the effective use of technology must include the topic of digital citizenship. Mike Ribble defines digital citizenship as "the continuously developing norms of appropriate, responsible, and empowered technology use" (Ribble, 2017). According to Ribble there are Nine Themes of Digital Citizenship. The first theme is digital access. This is the equitable distribution of technology and online resources. The recent development of COVID-19 and having to move all instruction online has made us very aware of the lack of digital access some students face. COVID-19 has also significantly impacted the second feature, digital commerce. This refers to the electronic buying and selling of goods in a digital setting, which has increased significantly because of stay-at-home rules.

The next three themes relate to how interactions occur in the digital setting. The third theme digital communication and collaboration refers to the how ideas are shared with others. The fourth, digital etiquette, refers to the procedures for consideration of others while using digital devices. The final theme in this category is digital fluency or the understanding of the technology and its use.

The last four themes relate to the social and legal ramifications of technology, which include (1) digital health and welfare that focuses on developing appropriate physical and psychological well-being in the digital world; (2) digital law which refers to the responsibility for actions and deeds in the online world and would include issues such as cyberbullying and sexting; (3) digital rights and responsibilities that deals with helping students understand that they have rights, but they also must protect others in the digital environment; and (4) digital security and privacy that involves the understanding of how to provide safety to others from viruses, worms, and other bots being passed along from one device to another.

Ribble believes these elements of digital citizenship should be part of every classroom, beginning in kindergarten and continuing through the educational experience. These should be presented through the concept of **REPs**—Respect, Educate, and Protect. It is important to note in viewing the elements discussed above how far digital citizenship extends beyond safe online practices.

Because nine elements can be a lot to remember, digital citizenship has simplified these into the three guiding principles of the S3 Framework. The first principle of Safety focuses on the importance of protecting yourself and others. The second principle, Savvy, focuses on the importance of educating yourself and connecting with others. The final principle, Social, emphasizes the importance of helping everyone make decisions to respect ourselves and others. These three facets work through the levels of protection, education, and respect for yourself and others (Digital Citizenship, 2020).

As an educational leader who is concerned about meeting the needs of all of her students, Latoya is particularly drawn to the ideas of Digital Access. How can her school and district ensure that all of her students have access to the digital tools of learning? Laptops? High-speed internet?

TEACHERS' ATTITUDES TOWARD ED TECH

Our principal, Latoya Williams, can feel confident about how receptive her teachers will be to learning more about the effective use of technology. A 2019 Gallup poll reported nearly nine in ten students report using digital learning tools in school at least a few days a week. Eight in ten teachers strongly agree or agree on the value of digital learning tools and an increased number see the value growing in the future (Calderon & Carlson, 2019). Latoya should be aware there is a gap regarding support for the increased use of digital learning tools in schools between principals and administrators (71 percent and 75 percent) and teachers (53 percent). The reason behind this hesitation is one of many areas Latoya will want to understand as she seeks to fulfill her supervisor's call to ensure her teachers use technology to make meaningful learning happen.

Table 2.1 ISTE Essential Conditions

Criteria	Missing	Novice	Basic	Proficient	Exceptional
Shared Vision					
Empowered Leaders					
Implementation Planning					
Consistent & Adequate Funding					
Equitable Access					
Skilled Personnel					
Ongoing Professional Learning					
Technical Support					
Curriculum Framework					
Student-Centered Learning					
Assessment and Evaluation					
Engaged Communities					
Support Policies					
Supportive External Context					

REFLECT AND APPLY ACTIVITIES

2.1 Evaluate your school's progress toward technology integration using the ISTE Essential Conditions (Table 2.1) as your criteria.

Complete a graphic organizer similar to Table 2.1, then write a reflection explaining your evaluation. Where are the gaps? What should be the priorities moving forward? In your response include both the graphic organizer and the reflection.

2.2 Create a brief reflective survey for your teachers to use to evaluate the use of technology in their classrooms. Incorporate questions that reflect SAMR, TPACK, and the ISTE Standards for teachers.

REFERENCES

Anderson, L. W., & Krathwohl, D. R. (2001). *A Taxonomy for Teaching, Learning, and Assessing: A Revision of Bloom's Taxonomy of Educational Objectives*. Longman.

Anderson, M. (2015, May 26). *SAMR is Not a Ladder, a Word of Warning* [Blog Post]. https://ictevangelist.com/samr-is-not-a-ladder-purposeful-use -of-tech/.

Calderon, V. J., & Carlson, M. (2019). *Educators Agree on the Value of Ed Tech.* https://www.gallup.com/education/266564/educators-agree-value-tec h.aspx.

Digital Citizenship. (2020). *Nine Elements.* https://www.digitalcitizenship.net/ nine-elements.html.

France, P. E. (2018). *What the SAMR Model May Be Missing.* https://www.eds urge.com/news/2018-10-18-what-the-samr-model-may-be-missing.

Garcia, A. (2014). *Teaching in the Connected Learning Classroom.* Digital Media and Learning Research Hub.

Gosset, S. (2020). *The Future of Education Technology.* https://builtin.com/ edtech/future-education-technology.

Hamilton, E. R., Rosenberg, J. M., & Akcaoglu, M. (2016). The substitution augmentation modification redefinition (SAMR) model: A critical review and suggestions for its use. *TechTrends: Linking Research and Practice to Improve Learning, 60*(5), 433–441.

Hirsh-Pasek, K., Zosh, J. M., Golinkoff, R. M., Gray, J. H., Robb, M. B., & Kaufman, J. (2015). Putting education in "educational" apps: Lessons from the science of learning. *Psychological Science in the Public Interest, 16*(1), 3–34.

International Society for Technology in Education. (2003). *ISTE Essential Conditions.* https://www.iste.org/standards/essential-conditions.

International Society for Technology in Education. (2018). *ISTE Standards for Education Leaders.* https://www.iste.org/standards/for-education-leaders.

Mishra, P. (2018). *Revised Version of TPACK Image.* https://punyamishra.com /2018/09/10/the-tpack-diagram-gets-an-upgrade.

Mishra, P., & Koehler, M. J. (2006). Technological pedagogical content knowledge: A framework for teacher knowledge. *Teachers College Record, 108*(6), 1017–1054. doi:10.1111/j.1467-9620.2006.00684.x.

Office of Educational Technology. (2020). *National Education Technology Plan.* http://tech.ed.gov/netp.

Puentedura, R. R. (2013, May 29). *SAMR: Moving from Enhancement to Transformation* [Web Log Post]. http://www.hippasus.com/rrpweblog/a rchives/000095.html.

Purcell, K., Heaps, A., Buchanan, J., & Friedrich, L. (2013). *How Teachers are Using Technology at Home and in Their Classrooms.* Pew Research Center's Internet & American Life Project.

Ribble, M. (2017). *Digital Citizenship: Using Technology Appropriately.* http: //www.digitalcitizenship.net/Nine_Elements.html.

U.S. Department of Education, Office of Educational Technology. (2017). *Reimagining the Role of Technology in Education: National Education Technology Plan Update.* https://tech.ed.gov/files/2017/01/NETP17.pdf.

Chapter 3

Instructional Interactives

Keya Mukherjee

Fifth-grade teacher Ms. Brenda Small read an article in the *EdTech* online magazine about students at a middle school in Seattle, Washington, who had crafted an award-winning digital story documenting the importance of digital equity. The documentary had caught the attention of the local school board, who responded by providing much-needed hotspots to the school district. The previous year Ms. Small had attended a local instructional technology conference, where she had participated in a workshop on digital storytelling (DS). The story on *EdTech* resonated with Brenda both because of her recent experiences with remote learning that revealed the digital inequity in her school community and because of the concept of a student-created digital story.

In recent days, Brenda had become aware of the challenges that families and students were facing with remote learning during the current pandemic school closures. She had learned that while the need for devices for families without digital devices could be met in her school community, internet access would take longer. She became aware that some families were parking at local businesses to connect with the internet; others were using cell phone hotspots which resulted in data shortages. As she worked on boxing Chromebooks for those families who had internet access but needed the device and study packets for those without the device and internet access, she thought she had the perfect opportunity to work on a DS project with her students to capture the experiences of remote learning.

She shared her idea and the story from *EdTech* about the award-winning digital story with her principal, who was excited about the idea. With the principal on her side, she approached the families and the students with the idea for the project. She asked her students and their families to take pictures and videos to document their daily experiences with remote learning.

With parental permission and working with her principal, she gathered the necessary paperwork and had the students and their parents take two to three photos or one-minute videos each day to capture their daily experiences. Ten students and their families agreed to work on the project. The students submitted their photos and videos to her via email which she stored on her password-protected computer. Each week as the photos poured in, she was surprised to see what the students were sharing. From the "No internet messages" on the screen because of their lack of internet connectivity to the parent in a van in the McDonald's parking lot, to the school on TV through the local cable carrier, there were a plethora of images that were powerful depictions of the digital inequity during remote online pandemic pedagogy.

Brenda dug through her files from the conference workshop that she had attended, and she found handouts on some tips and tricks and web resources on DS. After investigating these, she decided that simplifying and adapting the resources from the *Transformative Story* website would best fit the needs of her young, novice learners. She met with the students remotely and together they sorted and selected the pictures and videos and wrote the script. Using a creative and collaborative approach, the class created and launched their first digital story "My Digital Learning."

Based on the age and the expertise level of her students, and her own inexperience with DS, Brenda kept the process simple. The students used PowerPoint to assemble the pictures to tell the story and then used a free screen-recording software to record the story. Ms. Small helped with the audio and video editing in order to keep the digital story within four minutes. Her class launched their first digital story "The Inequity of Remote Learning." The enthusiasm with which they shared it with other students, their parents, the principal, and other school and district leaders was amazing. Never had she seen her students so excited about a school project!

DIGITAL ACCESS

Much like Ms. Small, enthusiastic and creative teachers in different schools across the country are trying various approaches to infuse technology into the curriculum by involving students to leverage different aspects of their teaching. According to the National Science Board (2018), since President Obama announced the ConnectED initiative, which pledged to connect 99 percent of American students to next-generation broadband and high-speed wireless in their schools and libraries by 2018, the country has made significant progress in reaching this goal. Currently there is an additional emphasis to leverage the power of the internet to rethink student learning in different ways (National Education Technology Plan, 2020). The percentage of school districts with high-speed broadband has increased from 30 percent in 2013 to 88 percent in 2016 (Education Superhighway, 2017). Although some gaps with digital access remain, the projected future bandwidth growth rate in schools and libraries of 65 percent per year (State K-12 Broadband Leadership, 2019), which will continue to provide more technology access in students. With more availability of devices and tools, integration of technology with innovative teaching practices becomes readily available. Despite connectivity issues with the internet in many parts of rural America, more students today are able to access the internet at home and at school than ever before. This access provides additional opportunities and potential for learning. What does this mean for teachers and learners?

Technology integration has been part of teacher preparation and training for a while; however, seamless integration has been a problem in many cases as computers, mobile devices, software applications, or the internet were not as readily available for daily classroom practices. According to Edutopia (2020), integration happens when students use technology daily, have access, and work with tools that match the task at hand, and are provided opportunity to build a deeper understanding of the content. Additionally, technology integration depends on the kinds of technology available, how much access one has to technology, and who is using the technology.

Although research and practice with technology show that there are many technologies that can be used effectively to engage students with instructors, teachers are often hesitant to enhance learning with technology because of the difficulties they encounter when using technology in the classroom. Mishra and Koehler (2009) and Harriman and Branch (2012) note that while teachers, like most of today's adults, are exposed to and aware of technology, in both their personal and professional lives, this use and access to technology does not equate to an inherent knowledge of the pedagogical use of technology. According to the Project Tomorrow's report (2015), 93 percent of surveyed district administrators say that the effective use of technology within instruction is important for achieving their school's or district's core mission of education and preparation of students. Parents' views closely parallel that of administrators with 84 percent of parents indicating that they view school technology use as a value for their child's learning, and two-thirds of middle school students (64 percent) agree that effective technology use increases their interest in what they are learning at school. When student expectations match learning opportunities, when they have access to technology, when they can create and collaborate with technology, then there is more engagement with learning.

In this chapter the focus is on three specific technology applications that are easy to use and can be effortlessly incorporated into teaching for all learners: DS, QR codes, and microlearning videos. These three technology applications for teaching have been chosen based on their accessibility in readily available devices, their ease of use, and the free or very low-cost investment with the software application associated with the tool. These tools are simple to use, so placing technology in the hands of the learner allows them to take an active role in their learning. Additionally, the tools provide teachers a way to collaborate with students and foster achievement in a learner-centered environment. The rationale for the choice of the tools will be discussed along with suggestions and evidence from practice.

DIGITAL STORYTELLING

Digital storytelling is extending the ancient art form of storytelling to a digital world using computer-based, film-making tools to tell stories. Various video editing software (e.g., iMovie for the Mac, Movie Maker for Windows, Microsoft's Photo Story) are used to bring a story to life and share it with a wider audience. Digital stories can be teacher-generated or student-created. The Center of Digital Storytelling has compiled seven elements to frame DS tasks: point of view, a dramatic question, emotional content, gift of your voice, power of the soundtrack, economy, and pacing. Robin and Pierson (2005) expanded and modified the original seven and added four additional elements in their framework to make them applicable to digital stories created by students. Both these frameworks have been used to develop many digital stories shared and showcased in the Storycenter, OER Commons, and Educational Uses of Digital Storytelling websites.

Although elements of digital story design provide general guidance for teachers on how to develop digital stories, knowing how to use a systematic approach to the design and develop digital stories is necessary to help teachers work with students. According to Kearney (2011), lack of knowledge of how to effectively develop digital stories could lead to unstructured decisions, so formalized pedagogical frameworks are needed to help teachers leverage desirable outcomes from DS project, without which there would be pedagogical challenges of working with an open-ended instructional tool. A review of early DS frameworks (Theodosakis, 2001; Hoban, 2009) provided digital stories development in phases that draw from film-making, and according to Kearney (2011), these early frameworks focused more on the technical aspects of developing video and did not focus as much on pedagogy.

Pedagogical Frameworks for DS

Three frameworks describing the process of DS will be discussed in the chapter. The Center of Digital Story (CDS) which started an arts movement around personal stories provided the original steps to DS. In subsequent years, Lambert (2010) revised the original steps to refine the steps as the genre evolved. He modified the steps to include what makes a story a digital story, and what makes a digital story a good digital story. The revised steps starts with helping the learner clarify what the story would be about, consider the meaning aspect of the story, identify key moments from within the story to depict in the video, choose the accompanying visuals, audio, and music for the story, do a final review based on the intended audience, and finally determine how the story will be disseminated. In his sequence of steps, Lambert brings together narrative structural elements with multimedia to produce digital stories. Several examples of how Lambert's work has been used can be seen in stories shared on Storycenter.org. Another framework based on the original steps from CDS was adapted by Robin and Pierson (2005), who expanded and modified the elements to make them applicable to digital stories created by students: the overall purpose of the story, the narrator's point of view, the dramatic question(s), the choice of content, the clarity of voice, the pacing of the narrative, the use of a meaningful audio soundtrack, the quality of the images, video and other multimedia elements, the economy of the story detail, and the use of correct grammar and language. A third framework for DS comes from Morra (2013) on the eight steps of DS with students:

Step 1: Idea generation
Step 2: Research/explore/learn
Step 3: Write the script
Step 4: Develop the storyboard or plan
Step 5: Gather images, audio, and video
Step 6: Arrange the pieces
Step 7: Share the story with the intended audience
Step 8: Reflect on the process and product

In all the models discussed here, the emphasis is on the learner and the pedagogy of storytelling. The learners, who are the storytellers, create content based on their personal stories or academic projects. According to Morra (2013), digital stories take students beyond traditional assignments by supporting their acquisition of the twenty-first-century skills of creating, communicating, and collaborating. All three frameworks share similarities in the sequential steps for creating digital stories. Lambert's background in theater and the arts and his association with media developers resulted in many digital stories that have a basis in awareness in building a just and healthy world. Robin and Morra's background as educators provides the frameworks to develop many digital stories across many different content areas. Lesson examples and lesson plans can be found in the Storycenter, Educational Uses of Digital Storytelling, OER Commons, and Samantha Morra's Digital Storytelling websites.

Practice with DS

Wong (2018) relayed stories of middle school students who in their broadcast and journalism class produced ten-minute news broadcast every two weeks, which were then shared with the whole school.

Students took turns constructing all parts of the production, from storyboarding and writing scripts to filming, editing, and being the on-air talent. In their project, the teacher guided them, but allowed students to make decisions with all aspects of the DS project. In the process, these students were not only collaborating and teaching each other but also interacting with the expert voice of the teacher. Advanced students in high school and middle school acquired technology skills with applications, such as Adobe Pro while younger and less advanced students used simpler video editing software such as Windows Movie Maker.

Students tend to be less daunted by online video creation as it has a dominant presence in their lives with the popularity and the presence of YouTube, TikTok, and other short video-making tools on social media and mobile devices. A teacher in Wong's (2018) article stated, students were smart, capable, and passionate, and when given the opportunity and the right tools, they can prove that they can do work at a high level.

Since DS is photo-based storytelling, a range of tools is available for the novice to the experienced learner. Microsoft's Sway, Adobe's Spark, Apple's iMovie provide easy entry into the digital publishing/visual storytelling realm. Other applications like Animoto, Powtoon, WeVideo, and YouTube provide avenues to create excellent video-based stories. In order to make DS effective, the project needs to start simple and the choice of tools need to be based on the comfort, ease, age, and experience of the learners as well as on the teacher's comfort, accessibility of programs, and cost. Since students are capable and eager to use technology, a motivated and enthusiastic teacher can work collaboratively with the students to use the tools to apply concepts of DS and take learning beyond traditional assignments. Along with integrating content, DS gives students the opportunity to learn with twenty-first-century tools and develop skills that are needed in the workplace.

USE OF QUICK RESPONSE (QR) CODES

Another technology that allows learners and teachers to work together to facilitate and engage learning is the QR code, which is a label that when read by an optical device provides information that is attached to the code. Most of us have seen or used these close cluster of dots, lines, and boxes placed within a square which when scanned with a phone or computer camera open up an audio recording, a video, or a document.

This cluster of dots, known as the QR code started in the automobile industry in 1994 to track automobile parts in factories, but nowadays they have a much broader purpose (Shin et al., 2012). They are used in businesses to unveil additional product information to customers, on business cards, and on resumes for networking. Another use of QR codes is seen in the textbook publishing industry, these QR codes are placed alongside instructional materials within the textbook to connect learners to external multimedia resources, or additional instructional materials. In the arts and humanities, QR codes are used in museums where a scan opens up detailed information about the display. How can this versatile technology, which works off a smart phone's camera, is used widely across many fields, is easy to use, makes information easily accessible, and is here to stay with the prolific growth of smartphone, be leveraged for learning?

QR Codes in the Classroom

According to Rikala and Kankaanranta (2014), since QR codes are not designed for the educational context, it is important for the teacher to understand that this simple technology can be used to unveil to the learner resources beyond the classroom context. As with all technology integration, the focus needs to be on the learner, the lesson, the need, and the pedagogy. Because QR codes work on any smart device with a camera, it links learners to an outside world and supports learning by allowing teachers to expand learners' experiences by bringing in events and tasks from real-world settings (Rikala & Kankaanranta, 2014). Just as a QR coded resource can expand students' horizons from things and information that are afar, so also it can allow students to learn and share resources from within their own community. They can learn from a teacher-created resource or create one of their own. By providing a communication gateway to the outside world and by connecting learners to resources, this easy to use and affordable technology allows for learning to be available as on-demand learning when the learners' need it.

True to the paradigm of a constructivist approach to learning, where the focus is on the learner constructing new knowledge based on what they know and what they come in contact with, Boschen (2020) says that her main reason to use QR codes with her students is that "it's easy to give students web addresses and allows them to be more independent.

I'm all about automating and releasing responsibility to my students as much as possible. I want to be the facilitator of learning, but not the one who tells them all the answers" (para. 5). With QR codes, students not only are consumers of learning but also become active participants during the learning process, when they can use the tool to share their best work from science, arts, or history projects; develop or complete fun learning activities, such as scavenger hunts; work on research projects; receive differentiated learning and homework support; participate in collaborative learning; and older learners can even share resumes or portfolios. The technology can help strengthen home-school connections and provide information for parents on various school-related topics (Miller, 2014; Walsh, 2014; Mauk, 2017).

Technology in education is most useful when they are related to learning outcomes, but also when it brings an element of fun for learners who have grown up with digital devices. While procuring computers and other devices may be cost-prohibitive, smartphones, or devices like iPad or tablets are more readily available and can be used for instruction. According to National Research Council (2000), learning through real-world contexts that provide children with opportunities to engage with instruction is not a new idea, as providing students concrete experiences through field trips, laboratories, and work-study programs has been an established practice. However, while these experiences are invaluable, QR codes place these activities at the heart of academic instruction rather than away from the classroom context. They can be easily incorporated into learning because of accessibility and ease of use with the technology. According to Mauk (2017), a fifth-grade teacher from Texas, "Ever since I started using QR codes with my fifth-grade students, it's made learning a lot more fun and interactive in my classroom" (para. 1). And according to Boschen (2020), "Finally, it's just plain fun. I mean, who doesn't love holding a device to a code and having it open a whole new world?" (para. 7).

Generating and Reading QR Codes

The technology required to read and create QR codes is readily available and easy to use. While QR code readers are most popularly associated with smartphones, a computer works just as well, as long as the computer has a camera. The QR code can either be held up to the camera for the code to appear on the page or the camera icon from the computer can be used to click the QR code image to open the resource. There are several readers available for smartphone use as well as on the computer, including a Chrome extension the QR Code Extension. Generating a QR code is easy through either a computer or a smartphone. Several popular free and easy to use QR code generators are available: QR Code Generator website, QR Code Monkey, and the Google Chrome extension the QR Code Generator. Embedded in each of these applications are directions on how to easily create codes. Much like with DS, students are savvy and eager to use technology, so a motivated teacher who wants to invest in innovative teaching practices with QR codes can integrate technology by placing this easy to use technology in the hands of the learner, and work collaboratively with them to extend learning experiences beyond traditional assignments.

MICROLEARNING VIDEOS

Often called "bite-sized learning," microlearning videos are popular in both corporate training and in e-learning contexts because of the flexibility and efficiency that it offers learners who are not bound to traditional, face-to-face approaches of learning and who want training to update their skills while maintaining day-to-day work performance. Conceptualized as small bursts or bite-sized pieces of video-based learning, this crossover concept between e-learning and mobile learning puts learning in small, just-in-time packages that a learner can access at will. With the growth in access to the internet in schools, there is increased investment in technology for assessments and computer-enhanced delivery.

Along with some of the other technology tools discussed earlier, short bursts of video-based microlearning is a valuable tool in the K-12 classroom because it allows the teacher to incorporate learning bites or small pieces of learning at teaching junctures to increase engagement and academic growth. Since microlearning videos use small digitally enhanced units of learning that target short-term learning goals, these micro pieces allow for quick instruction or review to increase retention of important skills, encourage engagement, and foster academic growth.

Although microlearning videos have gained recent popularity because they offer students fresh and innovative ways to learn, this form of instruction is not new and has been popular as long as video has been used for instructional purposes (Attea, 1970). Its popularity comes from its modular structure, where small pieces of learning can be linked to targeted learning outcomes or learner needs. At a time when there is much discussion about dwindling attention spans and endless diversions, mobile learning with microlearning video nuggets that have a three- to five-minute instructional window, which are tightly linked to a specific learning objective that are often action-oriented and deliver just-in-time learning in rich media formats provide enhancements and support to traditional learning.

For K-12 teachers working with students with shortened attention span, lecture and auditory presentations are not always effective methods for reaching these learners. Instead, providing a variety of brief multimedia educational experiences can be more effective because students tend to see value in technology-enhanced learning. Microlearning is an avenue that can address rapidly changing educational needs, current pressures for instant access to information, demands for mobile learning, and help with closing performance gaps. As in business training, so also in the K-12 classroom, microlearning videos can be created and used in many ways to support teaching in the content areas. In math class a simply created video with a voice-over PowerPoint or with screen-recording software can be used to present the problem of the day, in reading class a digital story or animated vocabulary flashcards can be used to address academic vocabulary, while in social studies a digitized timeline reviewing historical facts, tables, or graphs, and in science class digitally enhanced charts can provide opportunities to effectively review, teach, or differentiate instruction in a short instructional time. In order for microlearning videos to be meaningful and not random or loose pieces of disconnected learning, designing these videos need to be guided by frameworks, such as those identified by Torgenson (2017):

- Focusing on a single topic rather than focusing on the lesson's entire objectives will keep the microlearning video small. For example, working with a few academic vocabulary terms or learning the language of comparison in academic discussions would enable the teacher to establish a smaller outcome from the larger lesson objective.
- Focusing on small chunks or tasks will help learners better comprehend, retain, and remember the information. Instead of the whole

topic, the teacher needs to determine what is most important for the learners. An example of a strategic focus would be digitizing and animating a few flashcards with key academic vocabulary rather than including the whole story.

- Creating microlearning videos will cater to students' needs. Teachers need to be focused on creating videos that provide support, differentiate, or modify tasks to help the learner make progress toward the learning goal.
- Designing videos using a few simple graphic design principles, such an eye-catching text, will help create a connection for the learner. Using a repeated color palette, size, and type of fonts makes the information stand out as important and aligned.
- Incorporating visual images will help to convey more than words. Enhancing visual thinking through the strategic use of simple graphics, images, and illustrations will help create an attractive presentation and engage the learner.
- Narrating videos using informal but proper language will make the video more memorable.
- Keeping the videos within a two to three minutes long time length does not overwhelm the learner.

Creating Microlearning Videos

While movie making is a significant endeavor, creating microlearning videos is not. Microlearning videos can be created either as formal videos that are scripted, shot, and edited after being filmed or as simple screen recordings, easily created animated videos, or even footage from outside sources as long as copyright is not violated. The choice of video creation depends on time, budget, resources, and most important the learners' needs. However, as with any presentation, being focused on the topic is important. For a two- to three-minute video, a simple script will allow the narrator to stay on topic and avoid repetition. As microlearning videos are tied to learners' needs, when possible, examples that personalize the story will help the learner tune into the lesson. Using simple images and illustrations that promote visual thinking and grab the learners' attention will keep the microlearning video engaging. Another feature to keep learners motivated is implanting interactive elements, such as short, but fun knowledge checks at the end of the lesson or a simple, small game. Most importantly, when creating these short videos a talking-head stance should be avoided at all cost, where information is being read from bullet points on slides.

CONCLUSION

DS, QR codes, and microlearning videos have been introduced in this chapter to discuss innovative ways to integrate technology in learning, but more specifically ways in which technology can be put in the hands of the learner in a learner-centered classroom. Technology integration is a process and not a single event in the classroom. It is not about finding the quick fix that will transform learning, but one that starts with a vision, a desire to change, a commitment to learning, a willingness to engage in trial and error, a collaboration with students and teachers, and a trust that the process will result in student learning and academic achievement.

REFLECT AND APPLY ACTIVITIES

3.1 Compared to traditional written storytelling, what are some of the challenges and benefits, or possible drawbacks, of creating multimodal/multimedia stories using DS techniques?

3.2 Write a unit plan that will enable students in your classroom to explore writing personal narratives using DS. Using one of the frameworks discussed about DS, detail the steps that you will use with your students to help them develop and create a digital story. The lesson should reflect your original thinking. Include the grade and age level for the lesson, address both technical and language-related learning outcomes, address equipment and materials to be used, content selection, storyboard and scripting, image and video selection, incorporate details related to the pre-production, production, and post-production stages of the video development, adherence to copyright and fair use, learning outcome assessment, and any instructor sources or guides that might be needed to support the lesson.

3.3 Choose a topic and determine an enabling objective to develop a microlearning video. Plan your presentation, collect visuals to support content, write your script using a storytelling perspective, use PowerPoint to build your slides with simple graphic design with appropriate visuals. You can either import your PowerPoint into one of the following applications that you are familiar with: Adobe Spark, Jing, WeVideo, Animoto, or use screen-recording application like Screencast-o-matic to capture your story to build your microlearning video.

REFERENCES

Attea, W. J. (1970). VTR: In-service tool for improving instruction. *Educational Leadership, 28*(2), 147–150.

Boschen, J. (2020). *Using QR Codes in the Classroom to Enhance Learning*. https://www.whatihavelearnedteaching.com/using-qr-codes-in-the-cl assroom/.

Digital Storytelling. (2020). https://www.oercommons.org/browse?f.featured_topic=digital-storytelling.

Education Superhighway. (2017). *Education Superhighway's Second Annual Report on the State of Broadband Connectivity in America's Public Schools*. https://s3-us-west-1.amazonaws.com/esh-sots-pdfs/2016_national_report_K12_broadband.pdf.

Harriman, C. L. S., & Branch, R. M. (2012). *Aligning Digital Storytelling to the TPACK Framework: A Learning Experience for Pre-Service Teachers in a Learning-By-Designing Project*. http://www.edweek.org/media/teacher techusagesurveyresults.pdf.

Hug, T. (2004). *Micro Learning and Narration Exploring Possibilities of Utilization of Narrations and Storytelling for the Designing of "Micro Units" and Didactical Micro-Learning Arrangements*. file:///C:/Users/key a.mukherjee/Downloads/Micro_Learning_and_Narration_Exploring_poss ibiliti%20(2).pdf.

Hoban, G. (2009). *Facilitating Learner-Generated Animations with Slowmation*. https://pdfs.semanticscholar.org/1451/eeb0a3318767e4931de7db 2836ea2dee6f20.pdf?_ga=2.155930942.425341093.1590086149-1966 947899.1587660553.

Kearney, M. (2011). A learning design for student-generated digital storytelling. *Learning Media and Technology, 36*(2), 169–188.

Lambert, J. (2013). *Digital Storytelling: Capturing Lives, Creating Community* (4th ed.). Routledge.

Mauk, A. (2017). *8 Ways I Make Learning Fun by Using QR Codes in The Classroom*. https://www.weareteachers.com/qr-codes-in-the-classroom/.

Miller, A. (2011). *Twelve Ideas for Teaching with QR Codes.* https://www.edu topia.org/blog/QR-codes-teaching-andrew-miller.

Morra, S. (2013). *8 Steps to Great Digital Storytelling.* https://samanthamorr a.com/2013/06/05/edudemic-article-on-digital-storytelling/?unapproved= 4949&moderation-hash=cc61406d19ed1acfec1933579e99de66#comment -4949.

Mishra, P., & Koehler, M. J. (2006). Technological pedagogical content knowledge: A framework for integrating technology in teacher knowledge. *Teachers College Record, 108*(6), 1017–1054.

National Research Council. (2000). *How People Learn: Brain, Mind, Experience, and School: Expanded Edition.* The National Academies Press. doi:10.17226/9853.

National Science Board. (2018). *Instructional Technology and Digital Learning.* https://nsf.gov/statistics/2018/nsb20181/report/sections/elementary-an d-secondary-mathematics-and-science-education/instructional-technology -and-digital-learning.

National Educational Technology Plan. (2020). https://tech.ed.gov/netp/.

QR Code Generator Pro. (2020). https://www.qr-code-generator.com/guides/ how-to-create-a-qr-code/#how-to-create-basic-qr-code.

QR Code Generator. (n.d.). https://www.the-qrcode-generator.com/whats-a-qr -code.

QR Code Monkey. (n.d.). https://www.qrcode-monkey.com/.

Rikala, J., & Kankaanranta, M. (2014). *Blending Classroom Teaching and Learning with QR Codes.* https://files.eric.ed.gov/fulltext/ED557237.pdf.

Robin, B. R. (2006). *The Educational Uses of Digital Storytelling.* http://dig italstorytelling.coe.uh.edu/getting_started.html.

Robin, B. (2020). *Educational Uses of Digital Storytelling.* https://digitalstory telling.coe.uh.edu/index.cfm.

Robin, B., & McNeil, S. G. (2012). *What Educators Should Know About Teaching Digital Storytelling.* https://files.eric.ed.gov/fulltext/EJ996781.pdf.

Robin, B., & Pierson, M. (2005). A multilevel approach to using digital storytelling in the classroom. In C. Crawford et al. (Eds.), *Proceedings of Society for Information Technology & Teacher Education International Conference 2005* (pp. 708–716). Chesapeake, VA: AACE.

Shin, D.-H., Jung, J., & Chang, B.-H. (2012). The psychology behind QR codes: User experience perspective. *Computers in Human Behavior, 28*(4), 1417–1426.

Schuck, S., & Kearney, M. (2008). Classroom-based use of two educational technologies: A sociocultural perspective. *Contemporary Issues in Technology and Teacher Education, 8*(4), 394–406.

Smeda, N., Dakich, E., & Sharda, N. (2012) Transforming pedagogies through digital storytelling: Framework and methodology. *2nd Annual International Conference on Education & e-Learning (EeL 2012)*, Bali, Indonesia.

State K-12 Broadband Leadership. (2019). *Driving Connectivity, Access and Student Success.* https://www.setda.org/master/wp-content/uploads/2019/05/Broadband-State-Leadership-2019-Final-a.pdf.

Shulman, R. (2018). *EdTech Investments Rise to a Historical $9.5 Billion: What your Startup Needs to Know.* https://www.forbes.com/sites/robynshulman/2018/01/26/edtech-investments-rise-to-a-historical-9-5-billion-what-your-startup-needs-to-know/#72c5d4e53a38.

Story Center. (n.d.). https://www.storycenter.org/history.

Taylor, D. H. (2017, January 6). *Micro Learning: Advance or Fantasy?* [Blog Post]. https://www.linkedin.com/pulse/micro-learning-advance-fantasy-donald-h-taylor?trk=prof-post.

The QR Code Extension. (n.d.). https://chrome.google.com/webstore/detail/the-qr-code-extension/oijdcdmnjjgnnhgljmhkjlablaejfeeb?hl=en.

Torgerson, C. (2017). *Embracing Microlearning in Your Learning Ecosystem.* https://blog.insynctraining.com/modern-learning-resource-library/byte-embracing-microlearning-in-your-learning-ecosystem?success=true.

Theodosakis, N. (2001). *The Director in the Classroom: How Filmmaking Inspires Learning.* Tech4Learning.

Walsh, A. (2014). *25 Fun Ways to Use QR Codes for Teaching and Learning.* https://www.emergingedtech.com/2014/12/25-ways-to-use-qr-codes-for-teaching-learning/.

Wong, W. (2018). *Students Adopt Software to Create Digital Stories.* https://edtechmagazine.com/k12/article/2018/01/students-adopt-software-create-digital-stories.

Chapter 4

Learners as Producers and Responders

Maximizing Learners' Experiences through Technology

Alexandra Kanellis, Tammy Quick, and Georgina Rivera-Singletary

Mr. Thomas teaches fifth-grade social studies at Jenkins Elementary School. During his fifteen-year teaching career, Mr. Thomas has seen a significant increase in the technology usage in his class. When he began teaching, the teacher's computer was the only one in the classroom, so he would schedule his class in the computer lab once a month. He now had a set of Chromebooks large enough for every student to have one, so he could implement a new technology program whenever he wanted.

Although he is passionate about geography, he oftentimes finds his students are disinterested in learning about it. He wondered what he could do to make the topic more engaging. During his planning period, Mr. Thomas skimmed through his curriculum maps to begin planning for the next month. He noticed that the class would be focusing on the following Florida Standards:

S.S.5.G.1.2 Use latitude and longitude to locate places.
SS.5.G.1.In.b: Use a coordinate grid on a map to locate places.
SS.5.G.1.Su.b: Use a simple coordinate grid on a drawing to locate features.

Mr. Thomas believes that students learn best through active involvement and allowing students to demonstrate their learning.

After examining the standards, he identified methods students could use to demonstrate their proficiency. He developed his unit lesson plan and the expectations for each assignment. Mr. Thomas planned to have the students investigate the geographic features of a third world country of their choice. They will need to identify the latitude and longitude of the country and the location of famous places using a coordinate grid. As a challenge, students should identify one feature for peers to locate using the coordinate grid. Students will identify this information and use it to create a Scribble Map of their chosen country. They will share this information with their peers through a multimedia presentation.

During a two-week period, Mr. Thomas provided class time for the students to select their countries, conduct research, make their Scribble Map, and design their presentations. The students could choose to create their presentation in PowerPoint, iMovie, or NearPod. As students worked on gathering their information and constructing their maps, Mr. Thomas met with them to discuss their progress and their presentation formats.

During their fourth grade, many of the students had used PowerPoint when they studied Florida history. Since the students were comfortable with this format, many of them chose to use it for their world geography assignment. He encouraged them to think about using one of the other presentation options. A few students who were members of the after-school technology club chose to make iMovies. Only one student chose to explore NearPod. With each of these programs, students had the ability to insert text, graphics, audio, and visual information.

INTRODUCTION

Technology impacts many aspects of our world. Cell phones, iPods, iPads, laptops, and many more digital devices exist in homes across the nation. Instead of asking if one owns a digital device, the question becomes how many different types of electronic tools does the person own. Communication has been greatly enhanced through various forms of technology; instant messaging, social media, video apps, and the list goes on. Students in today's society have used technology since birth. They learned the alphabet and how to count while watching their favorite shows on some digital device. Students at all grade levels carry a cell phone with them the way that previous generations grew up wearing watches. Today's learners use cell phones to replace watches, televisions, calculators, notes, encyclopedias, and newspapers. For teens, the cell phone provides a means for being connected to the internet and friends through various social media platforms and texting applications, such as WhatsApp, Twitter, and TikTok (American University, 2018). Those ubiquitous devices easily make their way into schools and classrooms across the country. Consequently, educational institutions have had to decide on the appropriate way to handle these devices. When students have access to cell phones in the classroom, educators are finding themselves battling for attention as students' focus moves from the lesson to the recent notification that just lit up the cell phone screen. As a result, educators and researchers are asking if cell phones should be allowed in school and even if it is possible to find a balance between the use of the cell phone as a tool or a distraction (American University, 2018).

Many academic institutions have developed policies and procedures against cell phone use in the classroom and during school time. Teachers often complain about the students' inappropriate use of cell phones for videotaping others, capturing pictures of test items, watching movies or videos, texting friends, and listening to music during classroom instruction. Because of the prohibition on cell phone usage, school officials invest time addressing these infractions, teachers stop instruction to address the inappropriate behaviors, and students lose instructional time while being disciplined. If teachers instead incorporated digital technology and cell phones into classroom instruction, the results could be different.

In recent years, the integration of digital technology has helped to facilitate more effective classroom instruction. Digital learning technologies can support and innovate teaching (Fernández-Ferrer & Cano, 2016). When teachers incorporate technology in the classroom, they are entering the digital world in which their students live. Efforts to minimize the use of technology in the classroom should be exchanged for learning experiences facilitated by technology and its integration into classroom curriculum and instruction.

INTEGRATION OF TECHNOLOGY

Technology integration provides students with opportunities to learn, share, and demonstrate their understanding of grade-level standards as knowledge seekers, producers, and sharers of information. The integration of technology into instruction enables students to create, design, and have a choice in how they learn, engage, and share content. This increased engagement is evident in middle and secondary classrooms when technology is used to build knowledge in every content area. Technology, when used in small groups and with targeted goals, can also help build collaboration and improve social skills which are abilities valued by today's employers (Jackson, 2013).

Successful technology integration requires targeted and well-integrated resources in the K-12 classroom. Teachers must be well-trained and have the tools readily accessible for immediate use and integration into their daily instruction. Conscientious decisions need to be made about how the digital resources support the curriculum standards and student performance. For technology integration to be successful, students must be able to use the tools to help master the information or content, not just to learn about a new digital tool (Terada, 2020).

THEORETICAL BACKGROUND ABOUT LEARNERS AS PRODUCERS

Technology usage has increased exponentially in recent decades. Students who once were required to submit their assignments in their "best handwriting" are now being asked to use digital tools to demonstrate what they have learned. A survey of nearly 20,000 students from over 100 countries found that use of technology in schools worldwide continues to expand. Approximately 48 percent of the students reported that they used a desktop computer in the classroom. Forty-two percent indicated that they used smartphones while 33 percent reported using interactive whiteboards and 20 percent indicated that they used tablets. Technology usage was incorporated with more traditional modes for demonstrating knowledge, such as pen and paper (90 percent) and whiteboards (73 percent) (Bernstein, 2019).

However, this integration of technology does not automatically result in increased academic learning. School administrators and teachers must understand the ways in which technology integration can enhance students' educational experiences (Rose & Cook, 2006). Both the methods used to introduce the specific technology and students' own learning preferences impact how students learn. When learners are engaged in meaningful and relevant ways, they tend to devote more time and effort into the activity, which results in a deeper understanding of the content (Hung et al., 2004). Technology helps to build students' interest, and in most cases, they will work harder and stay focused longer. Reflecting on Mr. Thomas' geography assignment, he increased engagement by challenging students to create their own maps and multimedia presentations to demonstrate their understanding of the content.

Demonstrating proficiency and understanding of concepts are not new to teaching, even though, how students demonstrate their proficiency and understanding has changed. A goal of education is to enhance students' ability to create which is at the peak of Bloom's (1994) taxonomy of higher-order thinking (Eady & Lockyer, 2013). Including instructional activities that move up Bloom's taxonomy, students become more knowledgeable and skilled resulting in an improved understanding of the content they are learning (Fastiggi, 2020).

Twenty-first-century learners have grown up in a digital world. They are not able to recall a time when they did not have immediate access to digital devices. A wealth of information is at their fingertips through the World Wide Web where a single search provides an abundance of information on any topic. Educators are faced with the challenge of supporting students as they interact and use digital resources appropriately.

Many school districts across the United States have begun incorporating some form of technology integration into their curriculum. New websites, apps, and digital resources are added, and the list is enhanced regularly. The digital resources that are hot or trendy today may be obsolete or replaced by more efficient tools as technology advances. In the scenario, Mr. Thomas identified technology tools that would enhance student learning while expanding their knowledge of the standards and allowing them to share information about the country of their choice. Using technology for the sake of using technology is not beneficial to student learning. The tools must complement and enhance students' mastery of the standards. Research on multimedia learning has demonstrated more positive outcomes for students who learn from resources that effectively combine words and pictures, rather than from those that include words alone (Mayer, 2008).

DIGITAL RESOURCES

According to Edutopia (2007), successful technology resource use in the classroom occurs when "a child or a teacher doesn't stop to think that he or she is using a technology tool—it is second nature. And students are often more actively engaged in projects when technology tools are a seamless part of the learning process" (para. 2). Software companies are constantly developing new options and tools in an attempt to meet the needs of K–12 teachers and students.

Presentation Software

Numerous types of presentation software can be used by teachers to present content or by learners to demonstrate their content knowledge. Microsoft PowerPoint, Prezi, Keynote, and Google Slides are all digital tools that can be used to create presentations. Each has easy-to-use functions which allow students or teachers to upload text, graphics, and audio to share information with others. Each of these programs offers ready-to-use templates, a variety of fonts and icons, animation, and interactive elements.

Microsoft PowerPoint is a component of Microsoft Office, which is used by over 500 million people (Microsoft, 2017). Since it can be used by both Mac and PC users, most students have access to this program. The advantages of PowerPoint are that it is user-friendly, can generate handouts, and allows for customization. Prezi is a more recent addition to the family of presentation tools, joining in 2009. The program creates nonlinear presentations with zooming functions and is cloud-based so the presentation can be accessed from any location. Challenges are that there is a learning curve, you cannot print a handout to accompany your presentation, and the program is not fully customizable. Inexpensive Prezi paid plans are available for a monthly fee. Some individuals have complained of motion sickness when watching these presentations (Presentation Geeks, 2018). Keynote, like PowerPoint, offers a variety of fonts and templates to make creation easy and presentations can be easily transferred between devices through iCloud. The major drawback of this program is that in order to play a presentation you need a Mac operating system. However, Keynote is free on all Mac devices. Keynote cannot be used to create graphs or infographics. Google Slides is the most popular alternative to PowerPoint and is free with a Google account. The Google Slides program is a collaborative tool that allows for cooperative editing in real-time. Presentations can be shared, opened, and edited by multiple users simultaneously and users are able to see slide-by-slide and character-by-character changes as other collaborators make edits. All work is saved automatically on the Google servers (Velarde, 2016).

Nearpod is a web-based interactive slideshow tool that provides greater possibilities than the previous type of presentation software discussed. Using the Nearpod platform, content can be shared synchronously or asynchronously. The program allows for increased learner engagement through questions, polls, pictures, and 3D images in the presentation. In addition, simulations and field trips can be used to enhance learner understanding. Learner responses to these embedded items can be easily retrieved during the lesson or at a later date. Nearpod can be used on desktop computers, iPads, or Chromebooks. Many of the features are available free, but a few options require an additional purchase. A free version is available for teachers who want to present interactive lessons or have their students create content (Rogowski, 2018b).

Response Programs

A variety of digital tools are available to engage students in responding to content. Nearpod was discussed under presentation software, but it is also a program that can be used to encourage responses. Glogster, Padlet, Kahoot, and Plickers are some additional possibilities that can be used as response programs. Often these types of tools can give students who are less confident a voice to participate in classroom discussions and activities.

Glogster is a response program where learners can create interactive online posters called Glogs. A Glog contains multimedia elements such as images, videos, audio, and text that can be shared with others. Students can demonstrate their content knowledge through the construction of their Glog. A free version is available for teacher use. This version is limited to thirty student users. Additional purchase options are available based upon users' needs. Teachers should be aware that although creation is not difficult, video embedding may be a little difficult, and the creation of a Glog can be time-consuming. The Glogpedia contains a collection of Glogs on a variety of topics, some of these might not be appropriate for younger learners, so teachers need to screen the Glogs they are going to share (Trautman, 2015).

Gaming tools are a type of response system that can be used for assessment and to increase student engagement. Plickers, Kahoot, and

Padlet are examples of tools that can be used in this way. These games can be teacher- or student-created. Plickers might be a great option if technology within the classroom is limited. The program is a low-tech rapid-response tool for formative assessment. With this program, a multiple-choice question is posed by the teacher, and students respond by holding up the correct side of their four-sided response card to display their answer choice. This method allows for all students to respond, but because of the way the cards are constructed only the teacher using the digital program knows how each student responded. Only one digital device is needed to read the students' answer cards rather than requiring a device for each student as with other response systems. Free printable cards are available for teachers or pre-made cards can be purchased (Rogowski, 2018a).

Kahoot is a game-based student response platform that uses multiple-choice quizzes that can be accessed through a computer browser or a mobile device. This system, unlike Plickers, requires that teachers have a digital device for each student. Learners earn points based upon the speed and the correctness of their response. The program keeps track of the score and will identify the student with the most points. This program might not be the best choice for classes that have students with physical or processing difficulties (Weebly, n.d.)

Padlet is an online bulletin board that learners can access through a link where students can share and present information anonymously or with a name. Images, videos, text, and audio can be added to the board. Anyone who has the Padlet board open on a digital device can read what others are posting, which might present a challenge if learners choose to create inappropriate content. The free version is currently limited to three Padlets, but individual teachers or school districts may purchase a site license for their school (Renard, 2017).

Organizational Tools

ThingLink is an educational tool that makes it easy to organize instructional content. Students can upload images and tag content to their photos or drawings. These tags can link to websites, videos, maps, audio recordings, or other images. A free version is available for teachers who want to present interactive presentations while providing students with a platform for sharing information. The educational version of the tool features "channels" that can be used for specific projects and are only available to registered group members (Botula, 2016).

EVALUATING TECHNOLOGY RESOURCES

Program developers set out with the best intentions for creating innovative digital resources for consumers. Yet, teachers and school administrators must critique these programs to ensure they address the specific criteria set forth in the school district's technology plan. It is important to consider that if the tool is age-appropriate, then does it increase engagement, support the standards, is flexible, and whether there are support materials available (Eady & Locyer, 2013). Through the lesson in the scenario, Mr. Thomas structured his unit to encourage engagement through students' choice and active learning through his technology choices. Students' creativity, learning preferences, and content knowledge were evident through their multimedia presentations.

ASSESSMENT WITH TECHNOLOGY

Assessment of learning is an important consideration in instructional planning to ensure students are learning. There are many forms of assessment that teachers use in the classroom, such as formal, informal, summative, and progress scales (Marzano, 2019). These assessment tools are designed to drive instruction and to stay abreast of the progress the students are making in their learning. Formative assessments are especially vital for diagnosing and modifying instruction to make certain students are successful with meeting standards. Formative assessments have been linked to increased student achievement (Pellegrino & Quellmalz, 2010).

Undoubtedly, technology has changed how we assess students. The prevalence of using online testing has increased dramatically in the last decade. A 2016 Education Week Research Center survey found that 83 percent of the district or school leaders indicated their teachers were using one or more digital tools for conducting formative assessments (Molnar, 2017). Informal assessments can now be administered in a variety of ways, such as using polls, response walls, text message exchanges, and clickers. Using these methods teachers receive instant information about who understands the content and who does not. But formative assessments are not the only assessments administered online. Standardized assessments and high stakes testing that were typically paper and pencil are now being administered on digital devices.

TECHNOLOGY-BASED ASSESSMENT

Technology-based assignments require assessments that will guide the students in developing appropriate representations of their knowledge while also supporting achievement results of student learning. Technology-based assignments like online presentations, visual or graphics, and development of blogs or web quests can be assessed using tools on virtual platforms such as audio, video, or email as well as instant messaging or texting (Department of Education, Office of Educational Technology, n.d.). Collaborative projects are another form of assignment that will require the assessment of multiple components. Assigning students their own group page on a platform can be helpful for tracking work progress. Researchers in the field categorize project-based assignments as those that require authentic assessment. Authentic assessment "provides direct measures, captures constructive nature of learning, integrates teaching, learning, and assessments, and provides multiple ways of demonstration" (Nast in National Education Assessment, n.d.). Nast (n.d.) described authentic tasks as demonstrating, real-world, constructing knowledge, and providing for student choice. Authentic virtual classroom simulations and assessment are important for students because it gives them control of their own learning and allows them to use the technology that they are accustomed to using.

CONCLUSION

Digital resources encourage increased engagement, achievement, independence, and self-advocacy in the classroom. Student engagement is perhaps one of the most difficult items to manage in the classroom particularly when working with unmotivated or struggling learners. In recent times, the increased possibility of having digital devices in school has opened an entirely new world of teaching and learning possibilities. The technical knowledge that students bring to the classroom can be instrumental in building an interest in classroom instruction and curriculum. Instead of prohibiting students from using their digital devices in the classroom, it would be beneficial to incorporate them into instruction. Welcoming technology into classrooms instruction and embracing these practices will engage students (Kuntz, 2012). Students' level of creativity is enhanced when they are encouraged to take charge of their own learning and use creativity to make sense of the content.

Mr. Thomas and teachers across the world are providing students the means to create, share, use, and develop information; these skills will be essential as they prepare for college and career. The digital resources identified in this chapter, as well as many others, help build students' confidence to seek assistance, communicate with teachers and peers as well as meet short term and long-term learning goals.

REFLECT AND APPLY ACTIVITIES

4.1 Based on the information in this chapter, your personal experience, and, other scholarly resources, create a multimedia presentation to share with students' families about how content creation and assessment technology can be used in a K-5 or 6–12 classroom.

4.2 Choose one of the resources identified in this chapter that you have not used previously. Investigate that digital resources and identify the pros and cons of that resource. Provide an example of how it could be used effectively in the classroom.

REFERENCES

American University. (2018, September). *Should Cell Phones Be Allowed in School?* School of Education. https://soeonline.american.edu/blog/cell-phon es-in-school.

Bernstein, L. (2019, February). Snapshot of technology in the classroom in 2019. *EdTech.* https://edtechmagazine.com/k12/article/2019/02/new-global -survey-offers-snapshot-technology-classroom-2019.

Bloom, B. S. (1994). Reflections on the development and the use of the taxonomy. *Yearbook: National Society for the Study of Education, 92*(2), 1–8.

Botula, A. L. (2016, January). ThingLink. *Common Sense Education.* https://www.commonsense.org/education/website/thinglink.

Department of Education, Office of Educational Technology. (n.d). *Section 4: Measuring for Learning.* https://tech.ed.gov/netp/assessment/.

Eady, M. J., & Lockyer, L. (2013). *Tools for Learning: Technology and Teaching Strategies. Learning to Teach in the Primary School.* Queensland University of Technology, Australia. https://ro.uow.edu.au/cgi/viewcontent.cg i?referer=https://www.google.com/&httpsredir=1&article=1413&context= asdpapers;Tools.

Erstad, O. (2008). Changing assessment practices and the role of it. In J. Voogt & G. Knezek (Eds.), *International Handbook of Information Technology in Primary and Secondary Education. Springer International Handbook of Information Technology in Primary and Secondary Education, 20.* Springer.

Edutopia. (2007, November). *What is Successful Technology Integration?* Author. https://www.edutopia.org/technology-integration-guide-description.

Fastiggi, W. (2020). Applying Bloom's taxonomy to the classroom. *Technology for Learners.* https://technologyforlearners.com/applying-blooms-taxon omy-to-the-classroom/.

Fernández-Ferrer, M., & Cano, E. (2016). The influence of the internet for pedagogical innovation: Using twitter to promote online collaborative learning. *International Journal of Educational Technology in Higher Education, 13*(22). doi:10.1186/s41239-016-0021-2.

Hung, V. H. K., Keppell, M., & Jong, M. S. Y. (2004). Learners as producers: Using project based learning to enhance meaningful learning through digital video production. In R. Atkinson, C. McBeath, D. Jonas-Dwyer, & R. Phillips (Eds.), *Beyond the Comfort Zone: Proceedings of the 21st ASCILITE Conference* (pp. 428–436). Perth.

Jackson, S. (2014, December). Find out how technology promotes teamwork and collaboration in classroom. *Digital Citizenship.* https://www.commonse nse.org/education/articles/how-technology-can-encourage-student-collab oration.

Kuntz, B. (2012). Engaging students by embracing technology. *ASCD, 54*(6). http://www.ascd.org/publications/newsletters/education-update/jun12/vol54 /num06/Engage-Students-by-Embracing-Technology.aspx.

Nast, P. (n.d.). Authentic assessment toolbox. *National Education Association.* http://www.nea.org/tools/lessons/57730.htm.

Marzano, R. J. (2019). *The Handbook for the New Art and Science of Teaching.* Solution Tree Press.

Mayer, R. E. (2008). Applying the science of learning: Evidence-based principles for the design of multimedia instruction. *American Psychologist, 63*(8), 760–769.

Microsoft. (2017, May). Executives, PowerPoint 7 time: Set your priorities. *Present Better.* https://24slides.com/presentbetter/time-wasted-powerpoints/.

Molnar, M. (2017, May). Market is booming for digital formative assessments. *Education Week.* https://www.edweek.org/ew/articles/2017/05/24/market-is -booming-for-digital-formative-assessments.html.

Pellegrino, J. W., & Quellmalz, E. S. (2010). Perspectives on the integration of technology and assessment. *Journal of Research on Technology in Education, 43*(2), 119–134. https://doi-org.saintleo.idm.oclc.org/10.1080/1539 1523.2010.10782565.

Presentation Geeks. (2018, May). Prezi vs. PowerPoint: Which one is better? Author. https://presentationgeeks.com/prezi-vs-powerpoint/.

Renard, L. (2017, August 9). 30 creative ways to use Padlet for teachers and students. *Bookwidgets.* https://www.bookwidgets.com/blog/2017/08/30-c reative-ways-to-use-padlet-for-teachers-and-students.

Rogowski, M. (2018a, May). Plickers. *Common Sense Education.* https://www .commonsense.org/education/app/plickers.

Rogowski, M. (2018b, November). Nearpod. *Common Sense Education.* https ://www.commonsense.org/education/app/nearpod.

Shapley, K., Sheehan D., Maloney C., & Walker-Caranikas, F. (2011). Effects of technology immersion on middle school students learning opportunities and achievement. *The Journal of Education Research, 104*(5), 299–350.

Terada, Y. (2020, May). A powerful model for understanding good tech integration. *Edutopia.* https://www.edutopia.org/technology-integration-guide-i mplementation.

Trautman, S. (2015, July). Glogster. *Common Sense Education.* https://www .commonsense.org/education/website/glogster.

Velarde, O. (2016, January 4). Best presentation software: 10 PowerPoint alternatives: Teaching knowledge and creativity. *Visme.* https://visme.co/blo g/powerpoint-alternatives/.

Viorica-Torii, C., &Carmen, A. (2013). The impact of educational technology on the learning styles of students. *Social and Behavioral Sciences, 83*, 851–855.

Webb, M., &Gibson, D. (2015). Technology enhanced assessment in complex collaborative settings. *Education and Information Technology, 20*, 675–695. doi:10.1007/s10639-015-9413-5.

Weebly. (n.d.). Using Kahoot! as a classroom communication tool. https:// kahootinfo.weebly.com/.

Chapter 5

Supporting Learning for All Learners

Lauren Pantoja

Connie Marker, assistant principal at Carpenter Middle School, was on her first classroom observation of the morning. The science teacher, Mr. Harold, was well-liked by students, and always had engaging lessons. Today, he invited her to visit his classroom to observe a lesson he planned using a game-like program that had students virtually traversing a planet identifying the layers of earth and their qualities. As expected, the students were engaged.

The game was being projected, and Mr. Harold seemed to be monitoring who was ahead in what appeared to be a race on the big screen. Although Connie only spent about twenty minutes visiting, she was given the impression that the activity lasted the entire fifty-minute class period. After leaving the classroom, she looked up the grade-level standard and noted that students were to describe the layers of solid earth and should understand the processes that build up and break down the Earth's surfaces. When looking at the impact on student learning, engagement was high, but this brief snapshot had her questioning if the grade-level standard was being addressed. She wondered how Mr. Harold would assess students' understanding, and if this particular program was the best choice for teaching this standard and addressing the differing needs of his students. The school's science proficiency last year on the state exam was about 36 percent. This Title I school had many struggling learners, but they were not going to reach grade-level expectations if lessons did not address the grade-level standards.

Her next observation was in an eighth-grade algebra classroom, where the teacher had a class set of computers and used them daily. Mrs. Spencer, the algebra teacher, consistently used a district-purchased, instructional platform that incorporated many tools for both engagement and formative assessment. Today the students were individually solving a word problem using a "draw it" tool and then submitting it. The teacher was monitoring students' responses on her computer while projecting the student screen using a tablet. When the timer buzzed, the teacher shared anonymously, one of the student's answers and asked, "Do you agree or disagree with this solution to the problem? Turn and talk to your shoulder partner and be prepared to share your thoughts. You have 2 minutes." Mrs. Spencer walked around the room monitoring the conversations and then called on two different pairs of students to share their thinking. She did a quick poll after the pairs expressed their opinions and found that the class was unevenly divided in their thinking. She reviewed the solution for the class indicating the correct response. Mrs. Spencer then moved to another problem and the class repeated the procedure. After the second problem was complete, she assigned the class several problems in their textbook and called a small group of students over to a table with a large whiteboard. It took everyone a few minutes to get settled, and that was when Connie slipped out of the room. She stopped to make some notes about how Mrs. Spencer used the program to assess students' understanding and push their thinking. Connie made a note to ask a follow-up question about how Mrs. Spencer determined who would be called to the small group. Overall, Connie Marker was pleased. This was a positive example of using technology to differentiate instruction.

Although a few of the students were off task, many of them were the students that were called into small group. Perhaps their lack of engagement could be attributed to their lack of understanding. She felt certain that Mrs. Spencer used that small group time to check for understanding and provide Tier 2 instruction. This was also an excellent example of how technology could be used to support struggling learners.

This was Connie Marker's second year as an assistant principal at Carpenter Middle School. Principal D'Angelo made it very clear during her initial interview that the school had an abundance of technological resources and that his goal was to see that the resources were not just used in classrooms, but that they were used to support students' learning with a focus on supporting the struggling learners and English

Language Learners (ELLs) that were a large percentage of their student population. She accepted the position with the promise that as an administrator with a strong curriculum background she would support teachers with incorporating technology into their instruction to engage and support all learners, differentiate instruction, and enhance the curriculum.

As Principal D'Angelo indicated, Carpenter Middle School had an abundance of technology especially compared to Connie's previous middle school, and the technology was always checked out. That was a huge plus. Teachers clamored to use computers and tablets in their classrooms. However, the technology, although engaging, was not always being used to improve learning. The lessons where she observed it being used to differentiate instruction were far and few between. This week during their administrators' meeting, Principal D'Angelo asked for a report on the progress of the integration of the use of technology in classrooms. Connie was doing classroom walkthroughs daily to get a picture of technology usage at Carpenter Middle School.

Connie worked with the academic coach on a schedule for professional development that began last year with an introduction to the Substitution Augmentation Modification Redefinition (SAMR) model to guide teachers as they thought about why and how they were incorporating technology into their instruction. They spent much time examining student data to determine student needs, and looking at various websites, applications, extensions, and available platforms to support student learning. Perhaps it was time to revisit this professional development plan to include teachers who were effectively using technology to support struggling learners.

ROLE OF TECHNOLOGY IN SUPPORT OF STUDENT LEARNING

When interviewing Connie Marker for her position, Principal D'Angelo indicated that during his classroom walkthroughs students were mostly engaged while using technology. In his Title I school, where they had less than 50 percent proficiency on every state subject exam, he wanted to tap into technology as a resource to support learners, but not at the cost of teaching technology over the content. He made it very clear that technology use needed to enhance and improve instructional practices while helping students meet grade-level standards. He saw technology as an excellent resource to engage and support struggling learners as well as his proficient and accelerated learners. He was aware that his teachers were at varied levels of expertise in using technology to effectively impact instruction, and hired Connie Marker, an instructional leader with a strong curriculum and technology background, to lead that effort.

In today's classrooms, technology is being used regularly by most teachers and students. The question is not whether to use technology to support learning in this ever-growing technological world, since technology is a part of our world and we need to use it to help prepare students for their future in college and careers. The question is how can educators use technology effectively in their practice to realize its full benefits and provide authentic learning experiences.

The U.S. Department of Educational Technology (2017) asserts, "When carefully designed and thoughtfully applied, technology can accelerate, amplify and expand the impact of effective teaching practice. However, to be transformative, educators need to have the knowledge and skills to take full advantage of technology-rich learning environments" (p. 5)

The SAMR model for technology integration is a widely known and accepted tool that was developed by Dr. Ruben Puentedura to facilitate educators in selecting, using, and evaluating technology in education (Boll, 2015). The model can be divided into two broad categories: Enhancement and Transformation. The category of Enhancement includes the Substitution and Augmentation levels. The Substitution level is where technology acts as a direct tool substitute, with no functional change to the instruction. For example, this might include using a word processor rather than handwriting a paper.

Augmentation is also included in the Enhancement category. In an augmented lesson, technology provides a direct substitute with functional improvement. Augmentation would likely support a step up in rigor and engagement. It might involve using different word processing tools such as a thesaurus or grammar checks. Modification and Redefinition are included in the Transformation category. At the Modification stage, technology allows for a significant redesign of a task. Students working collaboratively to write their research project using a live document in Microsoft Word or Google Docs would be an excellent example. The final stage is Redefinition; the task would be impossible without technology. Possibly, the information that was originally presented in written form transforms into a filmed documentary (Gorman, 2015). To simplify SAMR (see figure 2.1), a popular graphic makes the analogy of Substitution to a cup of coffee, Augmentation to a latte, Modification to a caramel macchiato, and Redefinition to pumpkin spice (Boll, 2015). The SAMR model is an excellent tool to assist educators in making decisions for supporting learning with technology.

THEORETICAL BACKGROUND FOR USING TECHNOLOGY TO SUPPORT LEARNERS

Principal D'Angelo was determined to use technology to support learning in his school to help all students but felt that technology would particularly benefit his struggling learners. Silver-Pacuilla and Fleishman remind educators that, "Accessibility features in common technology applications can help struggling students make important connections— to the content, among ideas, among their own sensory modes of learning, and between their digital competencies and the curriculum" (p. 85). When incorporating technology into curriculum to support learning, it is important for teachers to consider the specific needs of the individual learner. Technology that supports students with disabilities can "take many forms, can have multiple purposes, and can frequently change as technology evolves" (Israel et al., 2014, p. 5). When we consider technology for students with disabilities, it is important to determine if the technology will help the student access curriculum and achieve the learning goal. If the student has an Individual Educational Plan (IEP) assistive technology might be identified (King-Sears et al., 2009) to help meet learning goals, standards, and to "level the playing field."

Technology is beneficial for all learners; however, roughly 20percent of students are not successful with Tier I core instruction despite good instructional practices and quality curriculum. It can be challenging for teachers to provide Tier 2 and Tier 3 interventions that target individual students' specific deficits, but technology offers tiered interventions via websites (Burns, 2020), and supplemental resources that are often included in the core curriculum.

Technology increases the effectiveness for ELLs' second language acquisition. It can provide opportunities for encouraging authentic interaction for our ELLs, providing content that is comprehensible, developing problem-solving skills, enhancing language skills, supporting various learning styles, and practicing English (Lin, 2009).

Technology used to enhance a lesson where the technology is beneficial to students, but not necessary for the students to function, is considered classroom technology (King-Sears et al., 2009). If it engages students and improves outcomes, then it is valuable. However, "technology should not be used independent of purposeful instructional goals" (King-Sears et al., 2011, p. 570). The purpose of instruction, whether with or without technology, is to advance students toward meeting a lesson's learning goals and applicable standards. When teachers make decisions to include technology in instruction, it is important to determine and analyze the value technology adds to the lesson.

TECHNOLOGY

Earlier in this chapter we discussed the SAMR model which can be used to support selection, use, and evaluation of instructional technology. King-Sears, Swanson, and Mainzer (2011) have proposed a decision-making framework to support teachers in making decisions to purposefully integrate technology into instruction in support of learning for all students, but particularly for students with disabilities. The framework, in fact, is general enough that it can support all content learning. Their framework is called TECH which represents:

Target students' needs and learning outcomes.
Examine technology choices, then determine what to use.
Create opportunities to integrate technology with other instructional activities.
Handle the implementation and monitor the students' learning.
(King-Sears et al., 2011)

This technology framework emphasizes the implementation of technology that directly supports students' needs to help them achieve instructional goals. Monitoring the impact on students' learning will definitely benefit our struggling learners but will also benefit all learners. Do we really want to use technology that does not impact learning? The TECH framework can help prevent that from happening. Also, integrating technology with other instructional activities eliminates the possibility of just letting technology do the teaching. Learners often need a variety of instructional techniques to keep them engaged, and the repetition of new knowledge in a variety of contexts helps to solidify the new learning. The TECH framework can be used to evaluate technology to determine if the digital resource will specifically address learners' needs. When we integrate technology, it should be purposeful, and we need to monitor students' learning to determine its effectiveness in helping students achieve learning goals.

Technology for Building and Assessing Prior Knowledge

When considering technology resources that will support our learners, consider how students learn. Learners connect new learning to what they know (Bruno, 2015). This means that teachers need to consider what students already know, perhaps through a pretest, anticipation guide, brainstorming chart, or a graphic organizer such as a KWL (What I know, What I want to know, What I learned), and either activate the knowledge or provide some background knowledge. This can help prevent students from being overwhelmed (Bruno, 2015), and will help to increase their understanding.

According to Marzano, (2004), "what students *already know* about the content is one of the strongest indicators of how well they will learn new information relative to the content" (p. 1). What students know helps them make sense of new knowledge. This is true for all students, but it is an important instructional strategy for struggling learners as well as ELLs. ELLs may not have the background knowledge or experiences to facilitate comprehension (Carver & Pantoja, 2019). Virtual reality apps and programs designed for education are engaging resources for building background knowledge. Programs like NearPod Field Trip can take students on virtual field trips to places like deserts, historical monuments, and university campuses where they will get to see a 360-degree visual of the site (Nearpod, 2020). Titans of Space is a virtual reality app on Google Play with a minimum cost that will enhance instruction of the solar system with a tour of the planets and stars in the galaxy (Haumpton, 2017). ThingLink (n.d.) has a free collection of virtual reality lessons for science and language arts for elementary students. These virtual reality apps can take students to places or build knowledge that will support students' understanding of varied content. There are many virtual reality apps available for students; these are just a few.

Another method for building students' knowledge is through the use of digitally enhanced paired texts or text sets. "Text sets are a collection of texts tightly focused on a specific topic. They may include varied genres (fiction, nonfiction, poetry, and so forth) and media (such as blogs, maps, photographs, art, primary-source documents, and audio recordings)" (Garrison, 2016, para. 2). Student Achievement Partners (2020) asserts that although text sets support all learners, they particularly support struggling learners with vocabulary and background knowledge deficits. There are many digital resources available to teachers in support of text sets. Student Achievement Partners (n.d.) offers text sets for grades K-12; many of the text sets are free, others are available for purchase. Common Lit (2020) offers text sets for grades 3–12, and the materials are free. Newsela (2020) includes a library of articles for grades 2–12; there is both a free and paid version. The paid version offers standards-aligned content and text sets. ReadWorks (2020) is free with materials for students from kindergarten to twelfth grade and offers paired texts.

If we are scaffolding struggling learners or ELLs, paired texts or text sets may be more accessible with Read Aloud apps or Read Aloud Extensions. The Google Extension, Read Aloud (2020), is a Chrome and Firefox free tool that converts text to audio; it can be used on a variety of websites including online textbooks, and it will allow students to hear a book written in English in a language of their choice. Audiobook Reader (2018) is a free download from Google Play that converts books that you download into audiobooks; this audio reader also supports multiple languages. Natural Reader (n.d.) is a web reader with free and premium voices; for unlimited use of the premium voices there is a subscription fee. This program reads webpages, Google Docs, emails, PDFs, Word documents, and more. Users drag and drop files into the program, select the voice, and press play. Audio files can also be converted to MP3 for on-the-go listening, and font size and color can be changed to support struggling learners The English language text can be converted to multiple languages.

When considering online resources for building background knowledge, the age-old resources of encyclopedias should not be ruled out; they are also available online. Education World (2001) examined eight online encyclopedias and found that they were generally for upper elementary students and above. Descriptions of six of these encyclopedias that would be helpful for building knowledge are listed here. *Britannica* is listed as the one of the best but is most appropriate for high school students and adults. *Funk and Wagnells Multimedia Encyclopedia* which includes a dictionary, thesaurus, world atlas, animal encyclopedia, and newsfeed, was found to be most appropriate for advanced middle and high school students. *Encarta Reference* which is a subsection of Microsoft Encarta is suitable for middle school, high school, and adults. *Excite Encyclopedia Electronica* has short, not in-depth, articles most useful for elementary and middle school students. *Infoplease* includes almanacs, a dictionary, and an atlas. *Infoplease* and *Columbia Encyclopedia* both provide concise information on a topic. They are appropriate for upper middle school and high school students. Carver and Pantoja (2019) remind us that ELLs might find these encyclopedia formats intimidating and suggest that *Simple English Wikipedia* would be a good resource for ELLs. *English Wikipedia* is not a scholarly source, but it will support students with limited English, younger students, or those who might struggle with reading (Knutson, 2018).

There are many electronic resources available to informally assess students' prior knowledge about a topic. Electronic response systems are ideal for assessing knowledge because you can collect the information quickly, in real-time with live results, and in many cases the information is immediately disaggregated by student. Socrative is a cloud-based assessment tool that can be accessed from any digital device. Using Socrative you can ask quick questions that are true or false, multiple-choice, or short answer. You can also create a quiz to collect information with an exit ticket or in a game format. Socrative has both a free and paid version and can be accessed with smartphones, tablets, and computers (Dyer, 2019). Poll Everywhere is a formative assessment, online resource that has a free version for K-12 and higher education; the free version allows for a limited number of participants. There is also a paid version that offers more features. Poll Everywhere (n.d.) has an opened-ended question feature that captures your data for sharing in a cloud (Dyer, 2019). Kahoot (2020) is an easy-to-use, game-based response system where points are rewarded based on correct responses and the speed of the response. Teachers can create questions or use questions from a bank. Data is generated that reports student's answers to every question and the points they were rewarded. There is both a free and paid version.

Padlet is an easy-to-use website that can be used to assess students' prior knowledge. Given a topic, students can work individually or collaboratively to think about what they know and share on a blank, electronic canvas (Dyer, 2019). The responses, which resemble sticky notes, can be arranged in multiple ways, such as grids, streams, maps, or timelines (Padlet, 2020). These are just a few electronic response systems that can be used to determine students' prior knowledge on a topic. These tools can provide valuable insight to inform an instructional plan and will support new learning by activating background knowledge.

Technology for Providing Feedback

Feedback whether face-to-face, handwritten, or through technology guides students' learning. Teachers can help students develop problem-solving and critical-thinking skills by providing specific feedback with clear directions for improving performance on a given task (Bruno, 2015). Effective feedback should foster a growth mindset by providing specific information that will assist students when revising or the next time they try the task. It should focus on the process, not the results, while supporting deeper learning (Saaris, 2016). "Technology has the potential to make course feedback better—more effective, more engaging, more timely—but that won't happen automatically" (Fiock & Garcia, 2020, para. 3).

Many instructors have feedback tools readily available to them through Learning Management Systems (LMS) their educational institutions are already using, such as Canvas, Google Classroom, Blackboard, or Desire2Learn (Fiock & Garcia, 2020). These platforms generally include document review tools for assignment feedback with tracked comments and highlighting, as well as text, audio, or video responses within the grade book. However, if instructors are not using a LMS, there are other technology resources available outside an LMS.

Audio and video tools can be used to provide specific feedback. Rubrics often provide feedback on general areas of need or excellence on an assignment, but if you want to go deeper and give specifics, a video tool will personalize your feedback. A screencast, which is a digital recording of what's on your computer screen, along with audio, is an excellent method for providing personalized commentary. There are many free screencast tools available. Quicktime (2020) is a free media player that is compatible with Macs; it offers video recording, screen recording, and audio recording. CamStudio (2019) is a free screen recording program for Windows. As with Quicktime (2020), you can record all or part of your screen, including a voiceover, and easily upload and share videos. CamStudio (2019) has both a free and paid version (Brown, 2020). Video conferencing is also an excellent personalized tool for providing feedback. You can have one-on-one conversations with students and share your computer screen or allow students to share their computer screens. During video conferencing you can also present polls, ask questions that require the use of thumbs up/down or yes/no icons, and monitor chat boxes for student responses. Giving immediate feedback is natural in this conversational setting. Zoom (2020) is a free video-conferencing resource that allows you to host up to 100 people for unlimited meetings, however, the free version has a 40-minute time limit for meetings.

As discussed earlier, there are many electronic response tools that allow an instructor to provide immediate feedback to students. Formative (2020) is a resource which allows a teacher to view all student responses as soon as they are submitted. Teachers can immediately leave real-time feedback in the form of a written comment. If students are struggling with a specific question or concept, the teacher can create a quick one-question assignment to gauge students' understanding and can provide whole class, small group, or individual feedback based on student responses. To support the entire group, teachers can anonymously display a student's response to a question (Miller, 2015) and use it to clarify errors in thinking or to affirm students' thinking. Formative (2020) is free, but also has paid versions. NearPod (n.d.) is also an interactive, electronic platform that provides opportunities for teachers to collect formative assessment data in a number of ways—open-ended questions, matching pairs, quizzes, polls, fill in the blanks, drawn responses, and more. Teachers can instantly view students' responses and can use the information to pull small groups to address misconceptions. FlipGrid (2020) is another interactive tool that is free to educators. Using FlipGrid (2020) teachers pose questions and students respond in short videos. Teachers and other students can post video feedback responses to the original videos. Even when using technology, the teacher is the most important factor in providing feedback. It is the teacher who provides specific, targeted feedback that supports students' learning. However, technology allows the teacher to use immediate data to make feedback informed and prompt.

Technology in Support of Collaboration

Learning is a social process. Renowned psychologist, Vygotsky's sociocultural theory stresses the importance of social interaction in the development of cognition (McLeod, 2018; Vygotsky, 1978). When students learn collaboratively it develops higher-level thinking skills, boosts confidence and self-esteem, teaches them how to work with others, and helps them develop leadership skills (Gates, 2018). This is particularly helpful for struggling learners.

Some electronic collaborative tools that are available to students include live documents. Microsoft Office and Google Docs both offer live word processing documents and presentation software that can be used for collaboration. Digital mind-mapping software can be used to help students organize their thinking and generally allows for collaboration. Popplet (2020) is a digital mind-mapping program that has a free and paid version, both versions allow for collaboration, but the paid version offers unlimited popplets. Coggle (n.d.) is also a mind-mapping software that supports collaboration. The free version offers unlimited public diagrams and three private diagrams. There are also several free software programs that support video collaboration such as Google Hangouts (2020), Skype (2019), and Zoom (2020).

Collaboration, even in an online learning environment, helps learners develop social skills. In order to solve academic problems, students in a collaborative setting are honing their communication skills. Collaboration also promotes learning from one another. Each student brings something to the collaborative table and this especially helps students understand different perspectives. Students might discuss and strategize to solve a problem or task but use a digital tool to produce the product or use the collaboration tool to provide feedback to one another throughout the process (Burns, 2018).

Technology in Support of Student Motivation and Engagement

There is a strong correlation between student engagement and student achievement across contents and at all levels of instruction (Dyer,

2015). Engagement can be described as being actively involved in learning. There is not one right answer to what an engaged learning environment looks like because an engaged learning environment can take many forms. According to Marzano, Pickering, and Heflebower (2011), to foster engagement, instructional decisions should be based on four questions. The first two questions focus on the attention of the students, "How do I feel?" and "Am I interested?" The last two questions, "Is this important?" and "Can I do this?" help to determine if the information will be remembered by the students. If the information is not of importance to students, they will not likely remember it. Finally, if students do not believe they can accomplish the task, their brains will reject the information (Marzano et al., 2011). To engage students, consider their interests, the relevance of the learning, and methods to support their success for any given task.

Today's students, who are often referred to as being "born digital" find the world of technology to be motivating (Chen, 2010). Incorporating digital games into the classroom creates interactive experiences that give every student an opportunity to participate, making it easier to accommodate students with disabilities (Chen, 2010). Ronimus et al. (2019) conducted a study of the effectiveness of a digital game on second-grade students who struggled with reading. Two groups of students received school-provided support, but only one of the groups received school support plus intervention with the digital game program. The results indicated that the game-based intervention was effective in supporting the students with reading difficulties; the intervention group developed faster word recognition than the control group. In addition, the students who were highly engaged in the intervention had higher gains in word and sentence reading fluency than those who were less engaged.

One example of a gaming system that has been developed to support education is Minecraft. Minecraft reinforces the development of creativity, critical thinking, and collaboration (Ascione, 2018). Minecraft allows players to build a 3D world out of blocks and is "so open-ended, in fact, that some refer to it as a platform instead of a game, or an 'infinite Lego set'" (Kamenetz, 2017, para. 4). Minecraft can be used to support every content. Students can connect worlds they build in Minecraft to novels or topics they are reading and writing about in language arts; they can recreate historical sites or events; they can create math projects related to volume, area, and perimeter (Ascione, 2018); and in science, they can identify how chemical reactions in the Minecraft World compare to that of the real world (Minecraft, 2020).

Classcraft is a cloud-based platform for the classroom that teachers can customize to promote classroom behaviors. The teacher may choose to use it to motivate students to complete assignments, do homework, engage in classroom activities, help others, or to work toward any other desired behaviors. It is available as both a web and mobile application (Sanchez, Young, & Jouneau-Sion, 2016). "The game acts as an augmented reality in the sense that there is no 3D game world; rather, the game world is real life, with the game acting as a digital layer on top of it" (Sanchez et al., 2016, p. 500). Teachers can form teams, create an avatar for each student, and assign powers and points for specific activities. The initial startup of the game requires considerable planning on the teacher's part, but the game is adaptable to the classroom setting and students' needs (Sanchez et al., 2016). Video games are a part of the culture of today's youth; the popularity of video games affords clues into students' preferred modes of interaction, collaboration, and participation (Cipollone et al., 2014). Technological resources whether used to engage students in topics or desired classroom behaviors are embraced by today's learners who have been "born digital."

LEARNING GOALS MATCHED TO TECHNOLOGY

Table 5.1 matches learning goals to possible technology choices, but this list is not exhaustive.

PROS AND CONS OF TECHNOLOGY TO SUPPORT ALL LEARNERS

More than once we have heard that technology is a double-edged sword; that it contributes to short attention spans and the lack of physical fitness (Chen, 2010). Technology can create barriers if not used properly. It can limit opportunities for human connection, collaboration, and have students buried in electronic screens rather than reaching out to peers or teachers (France, 2020). However, if the technology is used correctly, it can support collaboration in the classroom, and it can be used to enhance learning. If we are integrating technology with other

Table 5.1   Matching Learning Goals with Technology

Learning Goals	Technology	Resource Examples	Benefits to students
Building and Assessing Prior Knowledge			Connect new to known increasing engagement
	Virtual Reality	NearPod Field Trip ThingLink Virtual Reality Titans of Space	Builds knowledge with visuals
	Text Sets	ELA Literacy Lessons /Achieve the Core Common Lit Newsela ReadWorks	Builds knowledge and vocabulary
	Oral reading, text-to-speech	Read Aloud Extension Audio Book Reader, Google Play *Natural Reader*	Supports struggling readers with building background knowledge
	Electronic Encyclopedias	*Britannica* *Infoplease* and *Columbia Encyclopedia* *Funk & Wagnells Multimedia Encyclopedia* *Encarta Reference* *Excite Encyclopedia Electronica* *English Wikipedia*	Builds knowledge and vocabulary
	Electronic Response Systems	Socrative Poll Everywhere Kahoot Padlet	Assessing Prior Knowledge
Feedback			Guides student learning
	Learning Management Systems	Canvas Google Classroom Blackboard Desire2Learn	Guides student learning Built into Learning Management Systems
	Electronic Audio and Video Resources	Quicktime (for Mac) CamStudio (for PC)	Deeper, personalized feedback with specifics
	Video Conferencing	Zoom	One-on-one conversations
	Electronic Response Tools	Formative NearPod FlipGrid	Immediate feedback to students

(Continued)

Table 5.1   Matching Learning Goals with Technology (*Continued*)

Learning Goals	Technology	Resource Examples	Benefits to students
Collaboration			Supports critical thinking
	Electronic Collaborative Tools for Word Processing and Presentation	Google Docs Microsoft Office	Supports critical thinking, engagement, higher-level thinking, confidence, self-esteem, and leadership skills
	Mind-mapping Tools	Popplet Coggle	Supports critical thinking, engagement, higher-level thinking, confidence, self-esteem, and leadership skills
	Video Collaboration	Google Hangouts Skype Zoom	Supports critical thinking, engagement, higher-level thinking, confidence, self-esteem, and leadership skills
Motivation & Engagement			Every student participates
	Digital Games	*Minecraft* *Classcraft*	Gives every student an opportunity to participate Accommodations for students with disabilities

instructional activities, it will not inhibit students' attention spans or physical fitness. Good instruction is about balance and meeting the needs of students.

Silver-Pacuilla and Fleischman (2006) point out the benefits of technology to support all students including those who struggle with academic tasks. They spotlight technologies such as graphic organizers, speech recognition, text-to-speech, and e-resources as sound pedagogical practices that will help learners achieve success with academics and technology. There are customizable features in the digital text available to struggling learners that are not readily available in print text; the features available in digital text help learners develop independence (Scharaldi, 2020). Some examples of these supports are sites like Newsela which has varied levels of text of the same article, picture dictionaries, text-to-speech, and translate tools (Scharaldi, 2020). Also, consider how spell check supports the writing of students with a learning disability (Marino, 2009). Spell check levels the playing field for these students. If we implement technological resources to enhance learning and support, they will provide all students opportunities to learn and produce grade-level work.

CONCLUSION

Technology can be used to enhance and improve instructional practices if it is thoughtfully selected and supports students' acquisition of instructional goals. When making decisions to include technology in instruction, it is important to determine and analyze if the technology will add value to the lesson and support students' learning. Technology is used to support our struggling learners and all learners in multiple ways. It can be used to assess and build background knowledge—an important strategy for struggling learners because new learning is built on connections made to prior knowledge.

It can be used to provide immediate and specific feedback; feedback guides the learning process. Students learn from one another. Learning is a social activity and technology can be isolating, but it can also be collaborative, and collaboration provides peer support. Finally, technology can be used to engage and scaffold learners who may be disengage from academic tasks. Our youth are digital natives. They use technology daily, possibly hourly, tapping into the motivation that technology affords us in support of our learners will help them achieve. It is important to reiterate that technology does not replace exemplary instruction; technology enhances excellent instruction. The teacher is the number one factor in the success of any classroom, and thus it is important that instructional leaders such as Assistant Principal Connie Marker and Principal D'Angelo support teachers in understanding how to effectively embed technology into instruction to positively impact student achievement.

Table 5.2 TECH-Matching Technology to Needs

Name of Technology:

TECH   Rationale

Step 1: Target students' needs and learning outcomes.

What are the students' needs—e.g., reading fluency, writing,
vocabulary? Needs must match the learning outcome.

Step 2: Examine technology choices, then determine what to use.

Collaborate with others who are tech savvy.

Step 3: Create opportunities to integrate technology with other
instructional activities.

Integrate technology into other practices not just stand-alone.

Step 4: Handle the implementation and monitor the students'
learning.

Implemented how, when, and where? What evidence will be
used to monitor student progress?

REFLECT AND APPLY ACTIVITIES

5.1 Target a specific need in your educational setting for your learners. Using the table 5.2 for the TECH model, determine a digital tool that will address the need, how it will be integrated with other instructional activities, how it will be implemented, and how students' learning will be monitored.

5.2 Select and implement or observe a teacher implementing a technological resource with learners for collaborating, building background knowledge, providing feedback, and/or engaging students. What went well? What should be done differently the next time this resource is used? What did you observe about the impact the resource had on struggling learners or ELLs?

REFERENCES

Ascione, L. (2018). 7 ways Minecraft can make learning exciting again. *eSchool News.* https://www.eschoolnews.com/2018/11/27/7-ways-minecraft -can-make-learning-exciting-again/.

Audiobook Reader. (2018). *Goode Reader.* https://audioreader.goodereader .com/.

Boll, M. (Producer). (2015, April 10). Dr. Ruben Puentedura, creator of SAMR. *Education Vanguard,* Show #4 [Audio Podcast]. https://21clradio .com/education-vanguard-episode-4-dr-ruben-puentedura-creator-of-samr/.

Brown, M. D. (2000). Online encyclopedias: Which are the best ones for students? *Education World*. https://www.educationworld.com/a_tech/tech067 .shtml.

Bruno, P. (2015, October 9). How people learn: An evidence-based approach. *Edutopia*. https://www.edutopia.org/blog/how-people-learn-evidence-based -paul-bruno.

Burns, M. (2018, October 5). Why you should create a collaborative classroom this year. *Getting Smart*. https://www.gettingsmart.com/2018/10/why-you-should-create-a-collaborative-classroom-this-year/.

Burns, M. K. (2020). Using technology to enhance RtI implementation. *RTI Action Network*. http://www.rtinetwork.org/getstarted/implement/using-te chnology-to-enhance-rti-implementation.

CamStudio. (2019). https://camstudio.org/.

Carver, M., & Pantoja, L. (2019). Making a difference for ELLs with technology. *Florida Sunshine State TESOL Journal, 12*(2), 74–78.

Chen, M. (2010, September 16). If technology motivates students, let's use it! *Edutopia*. https://www.edutopia.org/blog/motivating-students-technology.

Cipollone, M., Schifter, C., & Moffat, R. A. (2014, March). Minecraft as a creative tool: A case study. *International Journal of Game-Based Learning, 4*(2), 1–14. https://www.researchgate.net/publication/287093943_Minecraft _as_a_creative_tool_A_case_study.

Coggle. (n.d.). https://coggle.it/.

CommonLit. (2020). https://www.commonlit.org/.

Dyer, K. (2015, September 17). Research proof points – better student engagement improves student learning. *NWEA*. https://www.nwea.org/blog/2015 /research-proof-points-better-student-engagement-improves-student-lear ning/.

Dyer, K. (2019, January 31). 75 digital tools and apps teachers can use to support formative assessment in the classroom. *Northwest Evaluation Association, NWEA*. https://www.nwea.org/blog/2019/75-digital-tools-apps-te achers-use-to-support-classroom-formative-assessment/.

Fiock, H., & Garcia, H. (2020). How to give your students better feedback with technology advice guide. *The Chronicle of Higher Education*. https://www .chronicle.com/interactives/20191108-Advice-Feedback.

Flipgrid. (2020). https://info.flipgrid.com/.

Formative. (2020). https://goformative.com/.

France, P. (2020, April 1). 3 tips for humanizing digital pedagogy. *Edutopia*. https://www.edutopia.org/article/3-tips-humanizing-digital-pedagogy.

Garrison, S. (2016, September 23). What are "text sets" and why use them in the classroom? *Thomas Fordham Institute*. https://fordhaminstitute.org/n ational/commentary/what-are-text-sets-and-why-use-them-classroom.

Gates, S. (2018, October 18). Benefits of collaboration. *neaToday*. http://nea today.org/new-educators/benefits-of-collaboration/.

Goldstein, D. (2020, March 13, updated 2020, March 17). Coronavirus is shutting schools. Is America ready for virtual learning? *The New York Times.* https://www.nytimes.com/2020/03/13/us/virtual-learning-challenges.html.

Google Hangouts. (2020). https://chrome.google.com/webstore/detail/google -hangouts/nckgahadagoaajjgafhacjanaoiihapd?hl=en.

Gorman, M. (2015, June 10). *Part 5 ... Beyond the Shine: Supporting Technology with the SAMR Model Plus Ten Great Resource Sites* [Blog Post]. https://blog.apastyle.org/apastyle/2016/04/how-to-cite-a-blog-post-in-apa-s tyle.html.

Haumpton, S. (2017, May 6). 7 top educational virtual reality apps. *Getting Smart.* https://www.gettingsmart.com/2017/05/7-best-educational-virtual-r eality-apps/.

Israel, M., Marino, M., Delisio, L., & Serianni, B. (2014). *Supporting Content Learning through Technology for K-12 Students with Disabilities (Document No. IC-10).* University Florida, Collaboration for Effective Educator, Development, Accountability, and Reform Center. https://ceedar.education.ufl.edu /wp-content/uploads/2014/09/IC-10_FINAL_09-10-14.pdf.

Joseph, M. (2020, April 6). COVID-19: Delivering special needs services at home. *DA District Administration.* https://districtadministration.com/covid -19-how-to-help-special-needs-students-continue-learning-at-home/.

Kahoot. (2020). https://kahoot.com/.

Kamenetz, A. (2017, August 9). 'Schoolifying' Minecraft without ruining it. *nprEd How Learning Happens.* https://www.npr.org/sections/ed/2017/08/09 /539518179/schoolifying-minecraft-without-ruining-it.

King-Sears, M. E., Swanson, C., & Mainzer, L. (2011). TECHnology and literacy for adolescents with disabilities. *Journal of Adolescent and Adult Literacy, 54*(8), 569–578.

Knutson, J. (2018, September 24). *How to Use Technology to Support ELLS in Your Classroom.* https://www.commonsense.org/education/articles/how-to -use-technology-to-support-ells-in-your-classroom.

Lin, L. (2009, May 15). *Technology and Second Language Learning.* https://fi les.eric.ed.gov/fulltext/ED505762.pdf.

Marzano, R. J. (2004). *Building Background Knowledge for Academic Achievement: Research on What Works in Schools.* Association for Supervision and Curriculum Development.

Marzano, R. J., Pickering, D., & Heflebower, T. (2011). *The Highly Engaged Classroom.* Marzano Research.

McLeod, S. (2018). Lev Vygotsky. *Simply Psychology.* https://www.simplyps ychology.org/vygotsky.html.

Marino, M. (2009). Understanding how adolescents with reading difficulties utilize technology-based tools. *Exceptionality, 17*(2), 88–102. doi:10.1080/09362830902805848.

Marino, M., Sameshima, P., & Beecher, C. (2009). Integrating TPACK in preservice teacher education: Frameworks for promoting inclusive educational practice. *Contemporary Issues in Technology and Teacher Education, 9*(2), 186–207.

Miller, M. (2015, December 7). 20 ways to use Formative for awesome assessment. *Ditch that Textbook.* https://ditchthattextbook.com/20-ways-to-use-formative-for-awesome-assessment/.

NaturalReader. (n.d.). NaturalSoft Ltd. https://www.naturalreaders.com/webapp.html.

NearPod. (n.d.). https://nearpod.com/.

Newsela, Inc. (2020). https://newsela.com/.

Poll Everywhere. (n.d.). https://www.polleverywhere.com/.

Popplet. (2020). https://apps.apple.com/us/app/popplet/id374151636.

QuickTime. (2020). https://support.apple.com/quicktime.

Read Aloud. (2020). Read aloud: A text to speech voice reader. *Lsdsoftware.* https://chrome.google.com/webstore/detail/read-aloud-a-text-to-spee/hd hinadidafjejdhmfkjgnolgimiaplp?hl=en.

ReadWorks. (2020). https://www.readworks.org/.

Ronimus, M., Eklund, K., Pesu, L., & Lyytinen, H. (2019, February 20). Supporting struggling learners with game-based learning. *Educational Technology Research and Development, 67*, 639–663.

Saaris, N. (2016, June 16). Effective feedback for deeper learning. *Actively Learning.* https://www.activelylearn.com/post/effective-feedback-for-dee per-learning.

Sanchez, E., Young, S., & Jouneau-Sion, C. (2017). Classcraft: From gamification to ludicization of classroom management. *Education and Information Technologies, 22*(2), 497–513. doi:http://dx.doi.org.saintleo.idm.oclc.org /10.1007/s10639-016-9489-6.

Scharaldi, K. (2020, January 30). Five reasons why struggling readers benefit from using technology. *Texthelp.* https://www.texthelp.com/en-gb/company /education-blog/november-2017/five-reasons-struggling-readers-benefit-fr om-tech/.

Silver-Pacuilla, H., & Fleischman, S. (2006, February). Research matters/ Technology to help struggling students. *Educational Leadership, 63*(5), 84–85. http://www.ascd.org/publications/educational-leadership/feb06/vol 63/num05/Technology-to-Help-Struggling-Students.aspx.

Skype. (2019). https://www.skype.com/en/.

Student Achievement Partners. (n.d.). Text set project: Building knowledge and vocabulary. *Achieve the Core.* https://achievethecore.org/page/2784/text-set -project-building-knowledge-and-vocabulary.

ThingLink. (n.d.). https://www.thinglink.com/.

U.S. Department of Education. Office of Educational Technology. (2017). *Reimagining the Role of Technology in Education*. http://tech.ed.gov.

Vygotsky, L. S. (1978). *Mind in Society: The Development of Higher Psychological Processes*. Harvard University Press. http://ouleft.org/wp-content/uploads/Vygotsky-Mind-in-Society.pdf.

Zoom. (2020). https://zoom.us/.

Chapter 6

Supporting Struggling Learners with Technology

Lin Carver

Monica White, academic coach at Explorer Elementary School, was anxious to visit Mr. Raymond's fourth grade room because he had just received an English Language Learner (ELL) who had arrived from China three weeks ago. Bohai, a reserved ten-year-old, was currently living with his parents in his aunt's home in the district. Neither his parents nor his aunt spoke much English, so Monica knew this was going to be a challenge. Mr. Raymond had already asked about materials written in Chinese, but the district did not have access to many of these. When Monica got to the classroom, she found Bohai sitting in the back of the room with headphones on working on an English language learning program.

This was a first step, but they needed to identify some extensions or digital options that could translate the information being used in class instruction into Chinese so that Mr. Raymond could help Bohai be able to participate in the class instruction. Knowing that it was important to get Bohai involved with the other students, Monica knew they had to find some more effective solutions to this problem.

As she continued to mull over this issue, she moved on to Mrs. Gallman's third grade classroom to see her reading/writing block. Monica had been told that students were ability-grouped and would be working in different centers around the room. One group of students, Mrs. Gallman's lowest group, were to be independently reading books, the next higher group was working on a spelling worksheet, while the other group was working at the table in the back with Mrs. Gallman during their reading group. As Monica watched the students, she noticed that the only group that seemed to be engaged was the group of students working with the teacher. Monica wondered if there were other options, especially for the lowest group of struggling students that might engage them more extensively.

The last class of the morning was one for students who had not reached proficiency on the state mathematics assessment the previous year. As she entered the room Monica noticed that each student was seated in front of a computer and completing individualized instruction as identified by their diagnostic assessment. Each student was working quietly and did not distract or interact with anyone else in the class. The classroom ran smoothly with each student completing the assigned work. The program seemed to be well structured to meet individual student needs, but the collaborative process seemed to be missing.

The school had already worked on ways to use data to inform instruction, but it looked like now would be the time to work highlighting various websites, applications, extensions, and available platforms to support struggling learners.

STRUGGLING LEARNERS' CRITICAL NEED

There is a critical need for teachers to support the ever-increasing number of at-risk learners. These learners would include ELLs, students with disabilities, and struggling learners. The National Assessment of Education Progress is used to track and compare academic achievement across the United States. The scores on the National Assessment of Educational Progress or NAEP are classified into four groups—below basic, basic, proficient, or advanced. Between the early 1990s and the late 2000s, students' mathematics achievement scores on the NAEP, improved, then they seemed to plateau. During the late 2000s reading scores also appeared to stagnate (USDOE, 2019).

Average students' scores remain well below what the test administrators consider to be "proficient" for each grade level. In reading, only 37 percent of fourth-graders and 36 percent of eighth-graders were classified as proficient. An even more alarming data point is that 67 percent of fourth graders scored below the proficient level in reading (Third Grade Literacy, 2018). In math, only 40 percent of fourth-graders and

33 percent of eighth-graders were able to perform at the proficient level (Barshay, 2018). The results from the NAEP determined that the average mathematics scores in 2019 were consistent with those in 2017. However, average 2019 reading scores decreased at grade 4 in approximately one-third of the states, and the eighth-grade scores were lower in more than half of the states (USDOE, 2019).

FACTORS AFFECTING ACHIEVEMENT LEVELS

In our K-12 schools, the growth in the number of ELLs has increased significantly and continues to expand. Between the years of 2009 and 2015 more than half of the states in the United States experienced an increase in the percentage of ELLs, while five states had an increase in the percentage of ELLs by over 40 percent (USDOE, 2017). During the 2015–2016 academic year, over 10 percent of the K-12 student population or 4,800,000 students were ELLs (USDOE, 2017). It is estimated that by the year 2030, about 40 percent of the U. S. school population will speak English as a second language (USDOE & N.I.C.H.D., 2003). Although ELLs come to our K-12 schools speaking many different first languages, almost three-fourths of the English language students in Florida are Castilian Spanish speakers. Other languages are represented in significantly smaller percentages (USDOE, 2017).

Students with disabilities currently represent 13.7 percent of the school age population which represented a slight, gradual increase from the 2001 level of 13.3 percent. The largest subgroup in exceptional student education is that of students with specific learning disabilities (NCES, 2019). Students with disabilities face many challenges as they attempt to reach the academic proficient level.

Students with physical disabilities represent a smaller subgroup of students with disabilities, but digital resources can help to level the playing field for these students as well. These students may experience difficulties with movement, posture, grasping or manipulating objects, communication, eating, perception, and/or reflex movements. These students may experience difficulty actually receiving information or they may have difficulty processing the information received. Both of these conditions will result in reading and writing difficulties. These students may have speech and language difficulties which make communication difficult (Anglophone, 2020).

Those students who are performing below grade level or at risk of performing below grade level face significant challenges in attempt to close the achievement gap. If these struggling students do not get additional support, they often lose motivation, fall further behind, score lower on high stakes exams and become at risk of dropping out (Frank, 2018).

ADDITIONAL SUPPORT FOR LEARNERS

To provide the needed language and academic support for our ELLs, students with disabilities, and struggling learners, teachers scaffold learning by providing opportunities for production experiences, building background knowledge, simplifying text features, and increasing learners' comprehension and fluency. Digital resources can help to address learners' needs while increasing students' engagement (Robertson, 2009). Infusing digital resources into instruction not only helps ELLs acquire a new language but also enhances motivation and confidence for all struggling learners (Lin, 2009).

Teachers can provide students with contextual cues to help expand or enhance their understanding of new concepts and ideas by using multimedia resources that incorporate pictures and/or videos. This visual or multimedia support can bridge the gap between everyday language and the more difficult content and academic language (Cruz, 2004). Digital resources not only help to increase understanding of the content being provided but also offer additional means for students to demonstrate their understanding of the content either orally or in writing (Brozek & Duckworth, n.d.).

Expressive Skills—Oral Language and Writing Production

"There are two key items ELLs need in order to improve their English—time and practice" (Robertson, 2009, para. 4), and there are engaging digital resources available to address these. Determining the needs of ELLs and students struggling with expressive language deficits helps instructors choose digital resources to support students' academic growth by providing additional opportunities for language production, background knowledge enhancement, complex text simplification, and fluency and comprehension expansion (Haneda & Wells, 2012).

Providing opportunities to discuss content topics while increasing opportunities for language production is an important consideration for all second language learners, students with disabilities, or struggling learners, whether these opportunities occur individually or with peers. These discussions improve text comprehension and argumentative writing skills (Buterbaugh, 2017). Often, instructors focus on teacher-directed classroom strategies that encourage vocabulary growth, collaboration, and graphic organizers (Uccelli et al., 2015) while overlooking digital resources that can be used to address these skills. Because of the prevalence of mobile devices, students have programs at their fingertips that can support learners with language related issues.

For second language learners, Duolingo is a free program used by more than 300 million individuals that can be used to create opportunities to hear, see, and construct written responses while translating from their native language to English. Learners select the amount of time they plan to spend daily practicing their new language skills. Students can learn new words which are introduced by category. The app includes both a visual and an audio component, and checks pronunciation. This simple, yet engaging, program provides the learner with immediate feedback. Ads occasionally pop up which can be distracting, but they help to keep the program free. Duolingo offers at least eighty-five different language courses in twenty-four languages (Duolingo, 2019).

For more advanced ELLs and struggling learners or who do not need the additional support of visuals but are still experiencing difficulty comprehending printed information, dictionary browser extensions might be particularly helpful. Extensions are small software programs that can modify and enhance the functionality of the browser. The dictionary extensions will provide the pronunciation and definition of an unknown word on a website simply by clicking on the printed word within the text. These extensions are available for Internet Explorer, Firefox, Chrome, and Safari browsers. The extension would need to be added to the specific computer the student is using.

Games and content creation are another way to provide opportunities for mastering academic language. Games can be an effective way to engage students from all backgrounds in learning new information and skills; BarryFunEnglish does just that. This online resource has a combination of visual and auditory flashcards. Premade or teacher created flashcard card sets can be used with sixteen different games including *The Memory Wheel, Battleship,* and *Speed* (BarryFunEnglish, 2017).

Collaborative tools such as VoiceThread, Teams, Zoom, and Skype provide unique opportunities for speaking, listening, and academic language practice. These can be used for enhancing student engagement and online presence. Instructors and students can create, share, and comment on images, presentations, videos, audio files, documents, and PDFs. Students can comment using a microphone, webcam, text, phone, and/or audio-file upload.

Flipgrid is a social learning platform where learners can practice and refine their content understanding. The "grid" or classroom is where educators ask a question and students can provide a video respond by creating a discussion around the given topic (Merrill, 2018). Flipgrid is free to all educators and can be used with multiple operating systems (Catalano, 2018).

Forms of social networking such as digital discussion boards can be beneficial for many struggling learners since they "encourage students to collaborate with others and participate in experiential learning experiences" while still allowing for extra processing time (Lacina, 2004, p. 114). These boards create a platform for students to be actively engaged in academic and social English outside of the classroom setting. These can be particularly beneficial because written responses occur asynchronously which allows struggling learners who need more time to process to compose their responses. Students' difficulty with processing speed may become evident through their difficulties processing verbal information, visual information, or through the speed of motor response (Braaten, 2020). The opportunity to respond asynchronously allows for addressing all of these concerns.

However, many struggling learners may experience difficulty getting their ideas into the appropriate written form. Google Docs Voice Typing can be used to make help students to overcome this difficulty. To activate this program in Google Doc, students should select "Voice Typing" from the dropdown Tools menu. This process opens up a microphone button that will change speech into printed text (Parrish, 2017). This program will allow students to focus on idea generation rather than spelling or grammatical structure. However, just providing additional language opportunities or writing support is not enough support for struggling learners.

BUILDING BACKGROUND KNOWLEDGE

Building a struggling learner's background knowledge is an important step because of the role it plays in enhancing content understanding. While lower vocabulary knowledge seems to be one factor that increases comprehension difficulties; lack of background knowledge also contributes to this challenge (Burgoyne et al., 2013). Complex texts place significant demands on readers because they require them to integrate their real-world knowledge with the printed content (Bowyer-Crane & Snowling, 2005). Learners may struggle because they lack the cultural and/or personal experiences for accessing the knowledge to help them comprehend the passage. Thus, differences in relevant background knowledge may negatively impact learners' comprehension of a complex text. NearPod Field Trip and Google Earth are engaging resources for building background knowledge. NearPod Field Trip program enables the teacher to create a virtual field trip. The teacher chooses a content slide, selects the Field Trip option, and indicates the desired destination which could be, for example, a physical location, an underwater locale, or even a position somewhere in space. Students are provided with a 360-degree visual of the site enabling students to develop an understanding of the setting.

Background knowledge can also be enhanced through reading about a topic in the encyclopedia; however, most struggling learners will find this academic format challenging. Simple English Wikipedia, although not a scholarly source, is an effective resource to use with some learners. It is a version of the Wikipedia that has been adapted for individuals who might struggle with reading academic texts (Knutson, 2018).

SIMPLIFYING COMPLEX TEXTS

Reading complex, academic texts can be challenging for any student, but it can be especially daunting for those who are struggling academically. Providing alternative ways of accessing key content texts and concepts allows struggling students to learn the same material as other students while continuing to develop their reading or English language skills thus providing access to grade level concepts (Ford, 2012). When printed materials are not available in the student's native language, Google Translate or the extension ImTranslator can be used to instantly translate words, phrases, and web pages between English and hundreds of other languages. Even though these programs do not always provide as accurate translation as may be desired depending on the dialect of the speaker, they can be used to provide immediate language support (Zeiger, 2014).

Complex texts provide significant challenges for struggling readers. Rewordify.com is a program that can be used to simplify difficult texts. Anything from a sentence, to a chapter, or an entire website can be copied and pasted into the text box. Then the student clicks the Rewordify text button and a simplified version appears instantly. The reworded portions of the text are highlighted allowing the learner to go back to hear, learn, and understand the original more difficult wording after reading the simplified version.

It is important for struggling learners to be exposed to the same content information as other learners. Newsela, an online group of news articles, scaffolds challenging texts by offering the same current event text written at five different Lexile levels. Even though the readability of the articles varies, the content of the article is similar allowing struggling learners to be exposed to the same content as other learners. English and Spanish nonfiction articles are available which cover a variety of topics: War & Peace, Science, Health, Kids, Money, Law, and Arts. The website content is updated daily from a wide range of sources, and all articles range from third to twelfth-grade readability. Each article features a quiz and writing prompt tailored to that specific content (Brereton, 2014).

Research indicates that visual information can provide a scaffold between everyday language and more difficult academic language (Cruz, 2004). Yang (2014) and Schmidt-Weigand and Scheiter (2011) determined that visual and auditory display models had a positive impact on struggling learners' content acquisition and confirmed that students learn more effectively when presented with content through dual codes rather than just a single code. Both studies found that the integration of verbal and visual imagery enhanced memory enabling learners in the experimental group to outperform their counterparts in the control group who learned using just printed material.

There are many ways to simplify a document or webpage. Numerous Chrome browser extensions are available that will enable second language, students with disabilities, and struggling learners to read text-heavy documents more easily. Mercury Reader is an extension that reduces the clutter on a webpage by deleting ads, sidebars, and other distractions. This extension might be particularly helpful for those students who are easily distracted or who have difficulty processing visual information. The extension reformats the document, so that the final version includes only the headlines and the content (not any advertisement or extraneous information) and the main articles are organized from left to right and top to bottom. Clicking on the gear icon in the upper-right corner of revised page will allow the reader to adjust the font style and size settings (Wong, 2016).

Another way to provide struggling learners access to the same information as other learners while decreasing reading demands is through a summary of the text. One Click Summarizer and TLDR (Too Long Didn't Read) are two of the many Chrome extensions that can be used to summary challenging information. With the One Click Summarizer, students select the amount of text they want summarized and paste it in the box. They then set the summary percentage to any amount from 10 to 90 percent and within seconds a summarized version of the text is read aloud to the student. One Click Summarizer easily reduces large amounts of information so that student spends less time reading the difficult text. The TLDR extension provides a condensed synopsis/summary view of news, blog posts, and other articles online. It can create summarized versions in four different lengths on any web page or web-based applications such as email and Evernote.

Enhancing Fluency and Comprehension

For many struggling learners, listening comprehension skills tend to be more fully developed than reading comprehension skills, consequently listening comprehension skills can be used to enhance reading comprehension and increase fluency. In the classroom a teacher read aloud can support listening and comprehension skills; however, a teacher is not always immediately available to provide this support. Read & Write is a Chrome extension that provides a read-aloud of the text for students who are not proficient readers. This program will read aloud documents (e.g., tests or quizzes) as well as websites. It can be used for whole text or portions of a text. In addition, for ELLs, it has translation and annotation features (ESL Nexus, 2019). The Chrome extension, Read Aloud, accomplishes the same function. It supports 40+ languages and reads a web page or article out loud with the option of highlighting the lines of text as they are being read. The voice is somewhat synthetic, but the pitch, speed and gender can be controlled (Isdsoftware.com, 2019).

CONCLUSION

Supporting struggling learners in the general education classroom can be a challenge. These learners may be ELLs who speak various languages and have varied social and cultural backgrounds and experiences. They may be students with specific physical or academic disabilities. They may be struggling readers who are experiencing difficulty with academic skills. They may have acquired adequate social language but may struggle with academic language. Advances in technology provide methods for addressing learners' needs while supporting teachers in meeting the demands of helping these learners be successful in their academic setting.

By providing additional support and opportunities for language production, simplifying texts and formats, enhancing vocabulary acquisition, and increasing background knowledge our struggling learners can become more successful in the K-12 educational setting. Finding time to support the unique needs of struggling learners can be difficult; technology can be used to support both the learners and the teachers. The challenge facing teachers lies in making classrooms places in which all students, even those who are struggling, have opportunities to learn and use language and printed texts for a wide variety of social and academic purposes. Providing a variety of academic and technological scaffolding will help to ensure all students' success.

REFLECT AND APPLY ACTIVITY

6.1 Find a digital program that is not currently being used in your setting to support a struggling learner. Explain the challenge that learner is facing and why this digital resource would help this particular learner. Explain how the resource operates and any costs involved.

6.2 Identify and compare two digital resources that your setting is not currently using to support students with the writing process. Explain the pros and cons of each and which students would most profit from each of the programs.

REFERENCES

Anglophone. (2020). Physical disabilities. *Supporting Students with Disabilities*. https://www2.unb.ca/alc/modules/physical-disabilities/myth-or-fact.html.

Barryfunenglish.com. (2017). BarryFunEnglish. https://barryfunenglish.com.

Barshay, J. (2018, April 10). *National Test Scores Reveal a Decade of Educational Stagnation.* https://hechingerreport.org/national-test-scores-reveal-a-decade-of-educational-stagnation/.

Bowyer-Crane, C., & Snowling, M. J. (2005). Assessing children's inference generation: What do tests of reading comprehension measure? *British Journal of Educational Psychology, 75,* 189–201. doi:10.1348/000708804X22674.

Braaten, E. (2020). Does processing speed vary from task to task? *Understood.* https://www.understood.org/en/learning-thinking-differences/child-learning-disabilities/information-processing-issues/does-processing-speed-vary-from-task-to-task.

Brereton, E. (2014). Newsela. *Common Sense Media.* https://www.commonsemedia.org/website-reviews/newsela.

Brozek, E., & Duckworth, D. (n.d.). Supporting English language learners through technology. *Educator's Voice, 4,* 10–15.

Burgoyne, K., Whiteley, H. E., & Hutchinson, J. M. (2013). The role of background knowledge in text comprehension for children learning English as an additional language. *Journal of Research in Reading, 36*(2), 132–148.

Buterbaugh, J. (2017, September 27). Quality talk increases critical thinking in high school STEM classrooms. *Penn State News.* https://news.psu.edu/story/484285/2017/09/27/academics/quality-talk-increases-critical-thinking-high-school-stem.

Catalano, F. (2018). Microsoft buys edtech startup Flipgrid and makes the video discussion tool free for all schools. *Geekwire.* https://www.geekwire.com/2018/microsoft-buys-edtech-startup-flipgrid-makes-video-discussion-tool-free-schools/.

Cruz, M. (2004). From the secondary section: Can English language learners acquire academic English? *The English Journal, 93*(4), 14–17.

Duolingo.com. (2019). Duolingo. https://www.duolingo.com.

ESL Nexus. (2019). 7 technology tools for newcomer ELLs. https://www.theeslnexus.com/2017/04/7-technology-tools-for-newcomer-ells.html.

Ford, K. (2012). Differentiated instruction for English Language Learners. *Colorin Colorado.* http://www.colorincolorado.org/article/differentiated-instruction-english-language-learners.

Frank, J. (2018, July 25). Meeting the needs of struggling students. *Apex Learning.* https://www.apexlearning.com/blog/innovation-struggling-students.

Haneda, M., & Wells, G. (2012). Some key pedagogic principles for helping ELLs to succeed in school. *Theory Into Practice, 51,* 297–304.

lsdsoftware.com. (2019). Read Aloud: A text to speech reader. https://chrome. google.com/webstore/detail/read-aloud-a-text-to-spee/hdhinadidafjejdhm fkjgnolgimiaplp.

Knutson, J. (2018, September 24). *How to Use Technology to Support ELLs in Your Classroom.* https://www.commonsense.org/education/blog/how-to-use -technology-to-support-ells-in-your-classroom.

Lacina, J. (Winter 2004). Promoting language acquisitions: Technology and English language learners. *Childhood Education, 81*(2), 113–115.

Lin, L. (2009). Technology and second language learning. *ERIC Document Reproduction Service No. ED505762.*

Merrill, J. (2018, July). Flipgrid – a social learning system. *The Techie Teacher.* https://www.thetechieteacher.net/2018/07/flipgrid-social-learning -platform.html.

National Center for Educational Statistics. (2019). *Students with Disabilities Fast Facts.* https://nces.ed.gov/fastfacts/display.asp?id=64.

Parrish, N. (2017, March 31). 5 Free assistive technology aids to use with struggling students. *Edutopia.* https://www.edutopia.org/discussion/five-free-assi stive-technology-aids-use-struggling-students.

Robertson, K. (2009). Five things teachers can do to improve learning for ELLs in the new year. *Reading Rockets.* http://www.readingrockets.org/article/five -things-teachers-can-do-improve-learning-ells-new-year.

Schmidt-Weigand, F., & Scheiter, K. (2011). The role of spatial description in learning from multimedia. *Computers in Human Behavior, 27*, 22–28.

Third Grade Literacy Fact Sheet. (2018). https://www.cfpciowa.org/docum ents/filelibrary/issues/school_readiness/8_things_docs/8_Things__1_F65 A08FA399B6.pdf.

Uccelli, P., Galloway, E. P., Barr, C. D., Meneses, A., & Dobbs, C. L. (2015). Proficiency and its association with reading comprehension. *Reading Research Quarterly, 50*(3), 337–356.

United States Department of Education (USDOE). (2019). Results from the 2019 mathematics and reading assessments. *The Nation's Report Card.* https://www.nationsreportcard.gov/mathematics/supportive_files/2019_in fographic.pdf.

United States Department of Education (USDOE). (2017). *Our Nation's English Learners.* https://www2.ed.gov/datastory/el-characteristics/index.html.

U.S. Department of Education (USDOE) & National Institute of Child Health and Human Development. (2003). *National Symposium on Learning Disabilities in English Language Learners.* Symposium Summary. Authors.

Wong, K. (2016). Mercury Reader for Chrome gives you a clean, ad-free view of articles on the web. *Lifehacker.com.* https://lifehacker.com/have-a-succe ssful-first-date-by-planning-the-same-first-1832623751.

Yang, H. (2014). Does multimedia support individual differences? EFL learners' listening comprehension and cognitive load. *Australasian Journal of Educational Technology, 30*(6), 699–713.

Zeiger, S. (2014). Google Translate. *Common Sense Education.* https://www.commonsense.org/education/website/google-translate.

Chapter 7

Evaluating Resources and Websites

Kevin Thomas and Donna Reeves-Brown

Sitting at her desk at Mill Creek Elementary school, Judy Runger excitedly turned on her new Google Chromebook. Judy, a fifth-grade teacher and team leader, has been teaching at Mill Creek for three years. Prior to coming to Mill Creek, she taught six years at another school in the district. When she arrived at Mill Creek, she immediately noticed a lack of technology in the school. Mill Creek is a Title 1 school with over 85 percent of its students receiving free/reduced lunch, which meant that many of the students did not have access to technology at home. This fact, Judy knew, made it imperative that Mill Creek students have access to technology at school so that they weren't in double jeopardy of falling into the digital divide. As a teacher leader, she met with her principal, Mrs. Everette, to discuss how Mill Creek could provide technology access to their students. Working with other school stakeholders, they developed a vision for technology integration for Mill Creek. The centerpiece of that vision was a 1:1 Chromebook initiative, and for the past two years, faculty, staff, students, and parents had been working to raise money. This year, with the assistance of matching funds from a local grocery store, the school was able to implement Phase 1 of the 1:1 initiative—classroom sets of Chromebooks for the fifth grade.

As the Chromebook powered on, Judy's first thought was "What app will I download?" She went to the Google Play store and perused some of the elementary school math applications (apps), reading reviews and ratings. Next, she googled "top 10 elementary math apps" and visited a couple of Pinterest pages on the topic. After about forty-five minutes of searching, she concluded that there were hundreds if not thousands of elementary math apps and that there did not seem to be a clear consensus on which were good and which were not. She thought to herself, "There has to be a better way to select instructional apps. There has to be some sort of app rubric." As a teacher leader, Judy decided to research rubrics for educational apps and to plan a professional development workshop to share her findings with her colleagues to assist them in identifying appropriate apps to use with students in their classrooms.

TEACHER TECHNOLOGY LEADERSHIP

As evidenced by her actions, Judy knows that technology creates additional responsibilities for teachers. Teachers have a responsibility to contribute to a shared vision of teaching and learning in their schools (EdTech Staff, 2017) that leverages technology as an accelerant (Sheninger & Murray, 2017). "Having a clear vision is essential, but so is testing every new idea against that vision" (Levin & Schum, 2012, p. 113). As one-to-one programs become more prevalent, teachers face challenges to modify their teaching practices to meet the needs of student-centered learning (Ertmer & Ottenbreit-Leftwich, 2013). However, some teachers move from aspiration to action more quickly than others (Rogers, 2003).

Technology has also placed new demands on teacher leaders like Judy. The role of teacher as technology leader is one that has emerged as a necessity in supporting technology integration in schools. Riel and Becker (2008) found that teacher leaders are ten times more likely to integrate technology as their traditional teaching colleagues are. As a result, teachers within the same school are often in various levels of development in their application of technology in the learning space. It makes sense that teachers who are struggling or need assistance in integrating technology turn to the teacher leader who is teaching next door.

The responsibilities of the teacher technology leader are very similar to that of a technology coach but perhaps less formal. Teachers collaborate with other educators to evaluate the effectiveness of digital learning content to inform decisions, to use particular apps and websites to support student learning (Standard 3c) (ISTE, 2019). These websites and apps are not add-ons to the curriculum but part of the curriculum itself.

TPACK FRAMEWORK AND ISTE STANDARDS

In planning for her professional development, Judy felt it was imperative to include both the TPACK framework and ISTE standards. Developed by Koehler and Mishra (2009), the TPACK framework builds on Shulman's theory (1987, 1986) on the interaction of pedagogical and content knowledge (PCK) (see figure 2.2). The TPACK model describes how "teachers' understanding of educational technologies and PCK interact with one another to produce effective teaching with technology" (p. 62). Evaluating educational apps and websites requires teachers to consider how the technology (T) assists them in teaching (P) the identified content (CK) to improve student learning. Of course, due to the differing nature of these technologies, the TPACK framework must be considered for each app and website.

The International Society for Technology in Education (ISTE) Standards provides teachers with a "framework for innovation in education" that is designed to assist educators in preparing "learners to thrive in work and life". Judy designed her app and website professional development to meet ISTE Educator Standards (EdTech Staff, 2017) by modeling for her colleagues the identification, exploration, evaluation, curation, and adoption of these technologies (Standard 2c), including authentic learning experiences that leverage these technologies (Standard 4a).

She also wanted to use these standards to provide her colleagues with a rationale for the adoption of apps and websites by connecting them to the ISTE Standards for Students (Team ISTE, 2016). For example, mobile technologies, like Chromebooks, can support meeting the diverse needs of all students by providing "equitable access to educational technology, digital content and learning opportunities" (Standard 2b). Research demonstrates that mobile technologies have the potential to differentiate instruction (Liu et al., 2014) and bridge the digital divide (Gherardi, 2016). Furthermore, by integrating mobile technologies, teachers are modeling the safe, legal, and ethical practices with digital tools (Standard 3c). In fact, some educators have indicated that the inappropriate use of mobile devices, in particular mobile phones by students is a direct result of the lack of modeling that should occur in schools (Thomas & McGee, 2012).

The use of mobile devices provides teachers an opportunity to demonstrate "cultural competency when communicating with students, parents and colleagues" (Standard 4d). Apps like Class Dojo and Remind allow teachers to communicate with students, parents/guardians, and school stakeholders via text messaging. Additionally, these apps have a feature that teachers can use to translate their messages into other languages. Students' use of mobile devices has also been linked to self-directed (Lindsey, 2016) and self-regulated (Bebell & O'Dwyer, 2010; Sha et al., 2012) learning, which fosters a classroom culture "where students take ownership of their learning goals and outcomes" (Standard 6a). Teachers can also use apps like Kahoot to implement formative and summative assessments (Standard 7b). Research has indicated that the gamification of instruction through the use of technologies like Kahoot can lead to increased engagement, motivation, and student learning (Wang, 2015).

IDENTIFYING AN EVALUATION RUBRIC

Judy's search of Google Play, the internet, and Pinterest yielded many elementary math websites and apps; however, it appeared to her that the selection process lacked a systematic, data driven methodology. She needed a validated evaluation tool, a rubric, to share with her colleagues and assist them in vetting the educational apps and websites that they would identify in their searches. She noted that after an exhaustive search, the website evaluation tools she could find were based on students looking for information, not for websites supporting learning in a particular content area. Judy noted that the apps and educational websites she used were very similar in their approaches to student learning. She wondered if this was why there were few rubrics specific to educational websites.

Perhaps the best rubric for teachers is the Evaluation Rubric for Mobile Apps created by Harry Walker (2013). Walker based his validated rubric on a review of the literature and consultation with experts in the use of mobile technologies in the classroom. There are several characteristics of Walker's rubric that make it the most suitable for teachers: applicability to all content areas, brevity, and shared criteria with other rubrics (table 7.1).

One of the primary benefits of Walker's rubric is its applicability. There are evaluation rubrics available to teachers who are attempting to identify apps designed for a specific grade level (Papadakis et al.,

Table 7.1 Harry Walker's Evaluation Rubric for Mobile Apps

Domain	4	3	2	1
Curriculum Connection	Skill(s) reinforced are strongly connected to the targeted skill or concept	Skill(s) reinforced are related to the targeted skill or concept	Skill(s) reinforced are prerequisite or foundation skills for the targeted skill or concept	Skill(s) reinforced are not clearly connected to the targeted skill or concept
Authenticity	Targeted skills are practiced in an authentic format/problem-based learning environment	Some aspects of the app are presented an authentic learning environment	Skills are practiced in a contrived game/ simulation format	Skills are practiced in rote or isolated fashion (e.g., flashcards)
Feedback	Feedback specific and results in improved student performance; data available electronically to student and teacher	Feedback is specific and results in improved performance (may include tutorial aids)	Feedback is limited to correctness of student responses and may allow for student to try again	Feedback is limited to correctness of student responses
Differentiation	App offers complete flexibility to alter settings to meet student needs	App offers more than one degree of flexibility to adjust settings to meet student needs	App offers limited flexibility (e.g., few levels such as easy, medium, hard)	App offers no flexibility (settings cannot be altered)
User Friendliness	Students can launch and navigate independently within the app	Students need to have the teacher review how to the use the app	Students need to have teacher review of how to the use the app on more than one occasion	Students need constant teacher supervision in order to use the app
Student Motivation	Students are highly motivated to use the app and select it as their first choice from a selection of related choices	Students will use the app as directed by the teacher	Students view the app as "more schoolwork" and may be off-task when directed by the teacher to use the app	Students avoid the use of the app or complain when the app is assigned by the teacher

Created by Harry Walker—Johns Hopkins University (2010).

2017), content area (Hirsh-Pasek et al., 2015), and/or student population (Israelson, 2015; Rosell-Auilar, 2017; Ok et al., 2016). However, Walker's rubric is applicable to all teachers.

Classroom teachers will also appreciate the length of Walker's rubric because it is a succinct one-page document. There are other rubrics that are designed to evaluate apps for all content areas. For example, Lee and Cherner (2015) developed the Evaluation Rubric for Educational Apps, which evaluates apps based on three domains: Instruction, Design, and Engagement and 24 dimensions; however, Lee and Cherner's rubric, which provides more specificity in its evaluation of apps, is eight pages long. Most teachers do not have the necessary time it takes to evaluate each app with an eight-page rubric. A list of possible app and website rubrics is located in table 7.2.

Finally, with the exception of one, all of the rubrics share the same six criteria as Walker's rubric: curriculum connection, authenticity, feedback, differentiation, user friendliness, and student motivation. Many of the rubrics also contained additional criteria not addressed in Walker's, for example, several identified costs (Papadakis et al., 2017; Rosell-Auilar, 2017), cultural sensitivity/bias free (Lee & Cherner, 2015; Ok et al., 2016), and cross platform compatibility (Lee & Kim, 2015; Lubniewski et al., 2018). A crosswalk comparing the various rubrics is provided in table 7.3.

As previously stated, Walker's rubric consists of six criteria: curriculum connection, authenticity, feedback, differentiation, user friendliness, and student motivation. In the area of *Curriculum Connections*, this rubric allows users to determine "how strongly the app correlates to a targeted skill from their curriculum" (Walker, 2013, p. 60). The *Authenticity* domain focuses on the quality of the student's experience when using the app. Quality is determined by the degree to which the app provides authentic learning experiences, which engage students in real world problems that connect new learning with prior knowledge. Next on the rubric is criteria for *Feedback*. As stated earlier, one of the benefits of student use of mobile applications is self-directed learning, which frees teachers to work with other students individually (Lindsey, 2016). To be effective, the app should provide quality feedback that is timely and constructive. The rubric facilitates reviewers in identifying two types of feedback. First, feedback should provide "branching based on student responses" and addresses "partially correct answers; that is, feedback serves to redirect students towards the

Table 7.2 List of App and Website Rubrics

Tool Name	Authors	Type of Apps	Features
Evaluation Rubric for iPod Apps	Walker, H. (2011). Evaluating the effectiveness of apps for mobile devices. (2011). *Journal of Special Education Technology*, 26(4), 59–63.	Educational Apps	1 page with 6 Criteria, Curriculum, Authenticity, Feedback, Differentiation, User Friendliness, Student Motivation. Rating 1–4
App Evaluation Rubric for Students with Learning Disabilities (LD)	Ok, M. W., Kim, M. K., Kang, E. Y., & Bryant, B. R. (2016). How to find good apps: An evaluation rubric for instructional apps for teaching students with learning disabilities. *Intervention in School and Clinic*, 51(4), 244–252.	Special Education Apps	Section 1: Basic Information Section 2: Objectives, Strategy, Examples, Practice, Error feedback, Error analysis, Progress monitoring, Motivation/ engagement, Visual and auditory stimuli, Font, Customization Section 3: Grading. Rating 1–3
Rubric for Evaluation of Educational Apps	Hirsh-Pasek, K., Zosh, J. M., Golinkoff, R. M., Gray, J. H., Robb, M. B., & Kaufman, J. (2015). Putting education in "educational" apps: Lessons from the science of learning. *Psychological Science in the Public Interest*, 16(1), 3–34.	Educational Apps	4 Criteria Active learning, Engaged Learning (3 subareas), Meaningful Learning, Socially Interactive Learning Rating: High, Medium, Low
Rubric for the Evaluation of Educational Apps for Preschool Children (REVEAC)	Papadakis, S., Kalogiannakis, M., & Zaranis, N. (2017). Designing and creating an educational app rubric for preschool teachers. *Education and Information Technologies*, 22, 3147–3165.	Preschool Apps	3-page rubric 4 Criteria: educational content, design, functionality, technology characteristics 19 sub-categories Rating 1–4

(*Continued*)

Table 7.2   List of App and Website Rubrics (Continued)

Tool Name	Authors	Type of Apps	Features
App evaluation rubric for school practitioners	Weng, P.-L., & Tabor-Doughty, T. (2015). Developing an app evaluation rubric for practitioners in special education. *Journal of Special Education Technology, 30*(1), 43–58.	iPad Apps	3-page rubric 11 Criteria: purpose, function, data, modalities, feedback, quality of feedback, design, content, usability, ability to be individualized, support, quality of support
Language Learning App Evaluation	Rosell-Auilar, F. (2017). State of the app: A taxonomy and framework for evaluating language learning mobile applications. *CALICO Journal, 34*(2), 243–258.	ELL Apps	1 page with 4 criteria Language (10 subareas) Pedagogy (9 subareas) User Experience (7 subareas) Technology (7 subareas)
The App Map	Israelson, M. H. (2015). The App Map: A tool for systematic evaluation of apps for early literacy learning. *The Reading Teacher, 69*(3), 339–349.	Early Literacy Apps	3 pages (Two Steps) 12 categories—8 early literacy skills: Rating Yes/No Four Criteria-Multimodal, literacy, intuitiveness, activity. Rating 1–4
Language Learning Mobile Application Evaluation Rubric	Chen, X. (2016). Language learning mobile app evaluation rubric. *Journal of Educational Technology Development Exchange, 9*(2), 39–51.	Adult ELL Apps	Content quality Pedagogical coherence, feedback and self-correction, motivation, usability, customization, sharing. Rating: 1–10
Evaluation Rubric for Educational Apps	Lee, C., & Cherner, T. (2015). A comprehensive evaluation rubric for assessing instructional apps. *Journal of Information Tech. Ed. Research, 14*, 21–53	Educational Apps	8 pages Three main criteria with twenty-four subareas Rating 1–5 and NA

(Continued)

Table 7.2   List of App and Website Rubrics (Continued)

Tool Name	Authors	Type of Apps	Features
App Checklist for Educators (ACE)	Lubniewski, K., McArthur, C., & Harriott, W. (2018). Evaluating instructional apps using the App Checklist for Educators (ACE). *International Electronic Journal of Elementary Education, 10*(3), 323–329.	Educational Apps	5-Step Evolution of twenty-five items Step 1: Age, Cost, Content, Targeted Skills, Step 2: Student Interest, Step 3: Design Features Step 4 Curriculum connection, Step 5: Instruction Features Rating: Yes/No (1 point for yes)
Evaluation Criteria for Educational Apps	Lee, J., & Kim, S. (2015). Validation of a tool evaluating educational apps for smart education. *Journal of Educational Computing Research, 52*(3), 435–450.	Gaming Apps for Smart Education	Teaching and Learning, Screen Design, Economy & Ethics Technology 4 criteria evaluated synchronous with more weight placed on instruction and technology.
S.P.I.D.E.R. website evaluation strategy	Johnson, T. (2011). S.P.I.D.E.R. a strategy for evaluating websites. *Library Media Connection, 29*(6), 58.	S.P.I.D.E.R. website evaluation	6 criteria source, purpose, information, domain, educational, reliability
Website evaluation criteria	Beck, S. E. (2009). *Evaluation Criteria from The Good, Bad & Ugly: or, Why It's a Good Idea to Evaluate Web Sources.*	Website	5 criteria authority, accuracy objectivity, currency, coverage
Implementing project SIED	Schmidt, M., Lin, M.-F., Paek, S., MacSuga-Gage, A., & Gage, N. A. (2017). Implementing project SIED, *Journal of Special Education Technology, 32*(1), 12–22.	Project Software Identification and Evaluation for Decision-Making (SIED)	4 criteria: assess need, product review, implement, evaluate 4 sub-actions in each area

Table 7.3 Crosswalk of Rubric Criteria

	Curriculum Connection	Authenticity	Feedback	Differentiation	User Friendliness	Student Motivation	Additional Criteria
Ok, M., Kim, M., Kang, E., & Bryant, B. (2016). How to find good apps: An evaluation rubric for instructional apps for teaching SWD. Intervention in School and Clinic, 51(4), 244–252.	x	-	x	x	x	x	• Bias
Hirsh-Pasek, K., Zosh, J., Golinkoff, R., Robb, M., & Kaufman, J. (2015). Psychological Science in the Public Interest, 16(1) 3–34. 32.	x	x	x	x	x	x	
Papadakis, S., Kalogiannakis, M., & Zaranis, N. (2017). Designing and creating an educational app rubric for preschool teachers. Education and Information Technologies, 22, 3147–3165.	x	x	x	x	x	x	• Social interactions • Bias free
Rosell-Auilar, F. (2017). State of the app: A taxonomy and framework for evaluating language learning mobile applications. Calico Journal, 34(2), 243–258.	x	x	x	x	x	x	-Price -Collaboration

Israelson, M. H. (2015). The App Map: A tool for systematic evaluation of apps for early literacy learning. *The Reading Teacher, 69*(3), 339–349.

Chen, X. (2016). Language learning mobile application evaluation rubric. *Journal of Educational Technology Development Exchange, 9*(2), 39–51.

Lee, C., & Cherner, T. (2015). A comprehensive evaluation rubric for assessing instructional apps. *Journal of Information Technology Education: Research, 14,* 21–53.

Lubniewski, K. L., McArthur, C. L., & Harriott, W. (2018). Evaluating instructional apps using the App Checklist for Educators (ACE). *International Electronic Journal of Elementary Education, 10*(3), 323–329.

Lee, J., & Kim, S. (2015). Validation of a tool evaluating educational apps for smart education. *Journal of Educational Computing Research, 52*(3), 435–450.

Reference							Additional criteria
Israelson, M. H. (2015).	x	x		x	x	x	
Chen, X. (2016).	x	x	x	x	x	x	
Lee, C., & Cherner, T. (2015).	x	x	x	x	x	x	• Cultural sensitivity • Collaborative
Lubniewski, K. L., McArthur, C. L., & Harriott, W. (2018).	x	x	x	x	x	x	• Cultural inclusive • Price • IEP goals
Lee, J., & Kim, S. (2015).	x	x	x	x	x	x	• Cost • Bias • Cross platform

correct response" (p. 61). Second, effective apps provide summative data on students' performance to both the student and the teacher. The timeliness of this feedback can assist teachers in making instructional decisions (Kay & LaSage, 2009). The usefulness of an app is also determined by its ability to differentiate instruction. *Differentiation* allows teachers and/or students to "control the level of difficulty" and "target specific skills," both of which can increase student success and motivation (p. 61). The last two domains are *Friendliness* and *Student Motivation*. The degree of friendliness is determined by how easy an app is for a student to use; this is often determined by the intuitiveness of the app's interface. The ease of use, novelty, and gamification as well as the level of student success all influence the level of motivation generated by an app. Interestingly price is intentionally not included as one of the domains because Walker does not see a correlation between price and the quality of an application.

What score does an app require to be considered good? Walker does not identify a specific score but does indicate that good apps should score a minimum of four (4) in the areas of Curriculum Connections, User Friendliness, and Student Motivation. When evaluating apps, Walker encourages teachers to simultaneously review a group of apps that are designed to address the same knowledge/skill, which allows the review to conduct a comparative analysis.

As Judy found during her initial search, there are numerous evaluation rubrics on the internet that have been developed by practitioners, instructional technologists, and other educational stakeholders. For example, Tony Vincent, a well-known educational technologist who created the Learning in Hand educational technology website, provides a number of rubrics on his website, including Harry Walker's; however, what often separates these rubrics from those presented above is that they are often not developed through empirical research. Furthermore, many of these rubrics, as is the case with two of the rubrics included on Tony Vincent's website (one developed by Vincent and the other by Kathy Schrock), are based on Harry Walker's rubric.

EVALUATION RUBRIC APPLICATION

In preparation for her professional development, Judy decided to test Harry Walker's rubric on a math app and a website that she had located and thought would be good to use with her students. She wanted to be sure to distinguish between using a website for reference and using a website to support learning, much like an app. Teachers needed to know how to evaluate both, but for this professional learning session she thought it would be best to stay with one rubric to demonstrate how both educational apps and educational websites could be evaluated using Walker's rubric.

The website Judy chose was Matific. It was a paid website, but teachers could get a free trial to see if they liked it. When Judy visited the website, it was easy to sign up for the trial. Judy started with the key components of Walker's rubric (see table 7.1), *curriculum connections*, *user friendliness*, and *student motivation*. If the website didn't get scores of four on these domains, there was no use in moving on. However, the *curriculum connection* was very strong. The games were directly connected to the Common Core standards. That made it easy to *differentiate* based on student needs. She scored curriculum connection a 4 as well as differentiation a 3.

The website seemed to be intuitive for students. She liked the gamification of the pirate map where the various game assignments could be found for each student. Students could follow the path and do the exercises in the order they appeared on the path to the treasure. This was certainly motivating for the students! Judy scored student motivation a 4. That meant that the three critical domains of curriculum connections, user friendliness, and student motivation had passed the first evaluation with differentiation as a bonus. So far, this website had real potential.

Contributing to the user friendliness of the website, students got three chances before an answer was declared an error. This was a plus for some of Judy's students. If they still didn't know the answer after three tries, the site showed students how to find the answer. Judy scored user friendliness a 4. Feedback seemed to be timely for students and teachers, so she scored feedback a 3.5 since there was a management component for teachers as well as students knowing whether their answers were correct. The only area left to evaluate was *authenticity*. She really considered the gamification a plus for student motivation, but when it came to *authenticity*, she had to admit that this website probably deserved a 2.

After considering the six domains in Walker's rubric, Judy found that Matific scored a 20.5 out of a possible score of 24. She felt the good features definitely outweighed the bad.

This website was worth trying with her students based on this evaluation.

Judy then moved to the app she planned to demonstrate. There was a lot of buzz about Prodigy among her colleagues, but Judy had never tried this app. When she downloaded the app and set up her teacher account, she understood why some of her colleagues liked the app so much. From the teacher's reporting perspective, Prodigy was incredible! It had a progress report for every student. It tracked student comprehension as well as student usage. There was a placement test so that students could practice their mathematics at the level they needed, and assignments and plans that the teacher could set up. "This is quite a comprehensive app!" thought Judy as she began to enroll a fake student and make an assignment on fractions.

In the critical areas of curriculum connections, user friendliness, and student motivation, Prodigy scored all 4s. The app could be modified to include specific targeted mathematics topics selected by the teacher for each student or group of students so there was definitely the ability to differentiate. Since different assignments could be customized and the program moved the student into more difficult material as the student succeeded, Judy scored differentiation a 3.

The app was easy for both teachers and students to use and the gamification made the learning fun. Judy wasn't sure if the app went too far in making the app fun, but she thought that might just improve student motivation. "Work a little, play a little," she decided. As far as the game, there was little authenticity, as students chose avatars, named them, cast spells and collected pets and gold. However, the way students generated the gold and energy was through authentic problem solving, so in the end, authenticity received a 4 as well. The final domain to be considered in Walker's rubric was feedback. There were teacher reports on student progress, comprehension, activity, among other reports that could be generated. Student feedback occurred within the game. Checking the rubric that meant feedback had a score of 4. The total for Prodigy on the Walker rubric was 23/24. This was an app that she would definitely use in her mathematics class!

Overall, Judy was happy with her selection of an app and a website to demonstrate for her professional learning session. She was more impressed that the Walker rubric was so straightforward and easy to use. Judy realized that she had evaluated two potential resources in just a short period of time. She was thrilled that she would be sharing a valuable resource that would help her colleagues choose appropriate materials for the students regardless of the tools they used.

REFLECT AND APPLY ACTIVITIES

7.1 Select an app or website you currently use in your classroom and describe the criteria that you used to select that app and compare these to Walker's rubric (see Table 7.1).

7.2 Using apps or websites that you have heard about or used with the learners that you work with, evaluate them using Walker's rubric and then compare the evaluation using a different rubric from the List of Educational App or Website Rubrics (see Table 7.2).

REFERENCES

Bebell, D., & O'Dwyer, L. M. (2010). Educational outcomes and research from 1:1 computing settings. *Journal of Technology, Learning, and Assessment, 9*(1), 5–15.

Beck, S. E. (2009). *Evaluation Criteria from The Good, The Bad & The Ugly: or, Why It's a Good Idea to Evaluate Web Sources.* http://lib.nmsu.edu/instr uction_backup/evalcrit.html.

Chen, X. (2016). Language learning mobile application evaluation rubric. *Journal of Educational Technology Development Exchange, 9*(2), 39–51.

EdTech Staff. (2017, June 26). ISTE 2017: New standards for educators focus on data, digital citizenship. https://edtechmagazine.com/k12/article/2017/06 /iste-2017-new-standards-educators-focus-data-digital-citizenship.

Fleischer, H. (2012). What is our current understanding of one-to-one computer projects: A systematic narrative research review. *Educational Research Review, 7*(107), 122. doi:10.1016/j.edurev.2011.11.004.

Gherardi, S. (2016). Social divides, digital bridges. In L. Miller, D. Becker, & K. Becker (Eds.), *Technology for Transformation: Perspectives of Hope in the Digital Age* (pp. 175–193). Information Age Publishing.

Hirsh-Pasek, K., Zosh, J. M., Golinkoff, R. M., Gray, J. H., Robb, M. B., & Kaufman, J. (2015). Putting education in "educational" apps: Lessons from the science of learning. *Psychological Science in the Public Interest, 16*(1), 3–34.

Israelson, M. H. (2015). The App Map: A tool for systematic evaluation of apps for early literacy learning. *The Reading Teacher, 69*(3), 339–349.

ISTE. (2019). ISTE Standards for coaches. https://www.iste.org/standards/ for-coaches.

Kay, R. H., & LaSage, A. (2009). Strategic assessment of audience response systems used in higher education. *Australasian Journal of Educational Technology, 25*(2), 235–249.

Koehler, M. J., & Mishra, P. (2009). What is technological pedagogical content knowledge? *Contemporary Issues in Technology and Teacher Education, 9*(1), 60–70.

Lai, C.-L., Hwang, G.-J., & Tu, Y.-H. (2018). The effects of computer-supported self-regulation in science inquiry on learning outcomes, learning processes, and self-efficacy. *Education Tech Research Development, 66,* 863–892. doi:10.1007/s11423-018-9585-y.

Lee, C. Y., & Cherner, T. (2015). A comprehensive evaluation rubric for assessing instructional apps. *Journal of Information Technology Education: Research, 14,* 21–53.

Lee, J., & Kim, S. (2015). Validation of a tool evaluating educational apps for smart education. *Journal of Educational Computing Research, 52*(3), 435–450.

Lindsay, L. (2016). Transformation of teacher practice using mobile technology with one-to-one classes: M-learning pedagogical approaches. *British Journal of Educational Technology, 47*(5), 883–892.

Liu, M., Scordino, R., Geurtz, R., Navarrete, C., Ko, Y. J., & Lim, M. H. (2014). A look at research on mobile learning in K-12 education from 2007 to present. *Journal of Research on Technology in Education, 46*(4), 325–372.

Lubniewski, K. L., McArthur, C. L., & Harriott, W. (2018). Evaluating instructional apps using the App Checklist for Educators (ACE). *International Electronic Journal of Elementary Education, 10*(3), 323–329.

Ok, M. W., Kim, M. K., Kang, E. Y., & Bryant, B. R. (2016). How to find good apps: An evaluation rubric for instructional apps for teaching students with learning disabilities. *Intervention in School and Clinic, 51*(4), 244–252.

Papadakis, S., Kalogiannakis, M., & Zaranis, N. (2017). Designing and creating an educational app rubric for preschool teachers. *Education and Information Technologies, 22,* 3147–3165.

Riel, M., & Becker, H. (2008). Characteristics of teacher leaders for information and communication technology. *International Handbook of Information Technology in Primary and Secondary Education, 20,* 397–417. doi:10.1007/978-0-387-73315-9_24.

Rogers, E. M. (2003). *Diffusion of Innovations* (5th ed.). New York, NY: Free Press.

Rosell-Auilar, F. (2017). State of the app: A taxonomy and framework for evaluating language learning mobile applications. *CALICO Journal, 34*(2), 243–258.

Schmidt, M. M., Lin, M.-F. G., Paek, S., MacSuga-Gage, A., & Gage, N. A. (2017). Implementing project SIED: Special education teachers' perceptions of a simplified technology decision-making process for app identification and evaluation. *Journal of Special Education Technology, 32*(1), 12–22.

Sha, L., Looi, C.-K., Chen, W., Seow, P., & Wong, L.-H. (2012). Recognizing and measuring self-regulated learning in a mobile learning environment. *Computers in Human Behavior, 28*(2), 718–728.

Sheninger, E. C., & Murray, T. C. (2017). *Learning Transformed: 8 Ways to Designing Tomorrow's Schools Today.* ASCD.

Shulman, L. (1986). Those who understand: Knowledge growth in teaching. *Educational Researcher, 15*(2), 4–14.

Shulman, L. S. (1987). Knowledge and teaching: Foundations of the new reform. *Harvard Educational Review, 57*(1), 1–22.

Team ISTE. (2016, June 26). The 2016 ISTE standards for students are here! https://www.iste.org/explore/ISTE-blog/The-2016-ISTE-Standards-for-Stu dents-are-here%21.

Thomas, K., & McGee, C. (2012). The only thing we have to fear is ... 120 characters. *Tech Trends, 56*(1), 19–33.

Walker, H. (2013). *Establishing Content Validity of an Evaluation Rubric for Mobile Technology Applications Utilizing the Delphi Method* (Unpublished Doctoral Dissertation). Johns Hopkins University, Baltimore, MD.

Wang, A. I. (2015). The wear out effect of a game-based student response system. *Computers & Education, 82*, 217–227.

Weng, P. L., & Tabor-Doughty, T. (2015). Developing an app evaluation rubric for practitioners in Special Education. *Journal of Special Education Technology, 30*(1), 43–58.

Chapter 8

Professional Development and Technology

Jodi Lamb

Jenn Smith is the new principal at Ocean Breeze Elementary School. Her school has struggled with technology integration even though there is ample technology and band width to support an instructional model with a heavy emphasis on digital tools. She decides to review the professional development opportunities that have been offered in the past to determine why implementation has not been wide-spread. As she reviewed the professional development plans and talked with her leadership team, it became clear that the approach used previously for professional development was not conducive to a successful, school-wide implementation. Jenn began to look for ways to hit the "re-start button" and help her faculty to learn how to effectively use all of the technology that was available.

To begin the investigation process, it will be helpful to have sufficient background knowledge about effective professional development models and how technology professional development differs from professional development on other topics.

PEDAGOGY VERSUS ANDRAGOGY VERSUS HEUTAGOGY

Pedagogy is the theory that guides children's learning. Students are dependent upon the teacher determining how, when, why, and on what learning will occur. Andragogy is the theory that guides adult learning. Adults have background knowledge and bring with them a set of experiences that may impact the new learning. They approach the learning differently than children do. Adult learning is based upon self-motivation and autonomy. The teacher is viewed more as a facilitator of the learning process. Heutagogy takes that to a different level for adults where learning is self-directed. The teacher provides resources, but the learning path and approach is up to the adult learner. This process hinges on adult self-efficacy and creativity (Heick, 2018). According to Chacko (2018), this should be seen as on the continuum with andragogy.

LEARNING THEORIES

Learning theories provide guidance or direction on how we choose to approach learning. The theories serve as a foundation for how an educator approaches learning. It is important to recognize that the three approaches listed below are important pieces of technology integration. If faculty members at a school do not prescribe to approaches like these, integration may be difficult.

Constructivism, found effective for all learners, "is the idea that learning is a social and collaborative process where cognitive development is possible through social interaction, collaboration, mentoring and exploring" (Psiopoulos et al., 2016, p. 209). This approach to learning is key in technology integration.

Transformational learning is where the "transformation occurs through a series of phases" usually caused by a "disorienting dilemma which is triggered by a life crisis or a major life transition, then progresses through self-examination and critical assessment of values, beliefs, and assumptions and results in a changed frame of reference from which to try to and ultimately adopt new ways of acting" (Psiropoulos, 2016, p. 211). It serves as a base for many professional development models.

In Experiential learning, educators "create learning experiences in the curricula to facilitate learning through discovery . . . [and it] fosters critical thinking, problem solving, and lifelong professional learning by encouraging learners to test out and apply new knowledge" (Chacko, 2018, p. 3). This approach is used effectively at all levels.

PROFESSIONAL DEVELOPMENT STANDARDS

In just the same way as there are content standards, there are also standards for professional development. Professional development providers should be attentive to the standards as they establish a plan for training and development. According to Hirsch and Hord (2018), "studying with and from peers has been shown to be a powerful learning design" (p. 1). It is clear that faculty can learn a tremendous amount from each other. There are key practices that should be in place to ensure a successful implementation and include clearly communicating the new vision, the plan to attain the new vision, the professional development to attain the vision, and the assistance necessary to successfully integrate the new technology and associated strategies.

A quick look at the Standards for Professional Learning (Learning Forward, 2011) highlights an emphasis on the practices that positively influences professional learning as a way to increase teacher effectiveness. These standards concentrate on elements such as leadership, learning communities, implementation, and outcomes. Additionally, Learning Forward offers four prerequisites necessary for professional learning to be effective. They are:

1. Educators who are committed to students, all students, is the foundation of effective professional learning
2. Each educator involved in professional learning comes to the experience ready to learn
3. Because there are disparate experience levels and use of practice among educators, professional learning can foster collaborative inquiry and learning that enhances individual and collective performance
4. Like all learners, educators learn in different ways and at different rates (p. 3).

MODELS OF PROFESSIONAL DEVELOPMENT

SRI Education, in their report regarding the ConnectEd Initiative, stated that the teachers involved in that initiative indicated that the professional development that was more hands-on with more follow up was more impactful than other professional development that had been delivered in more traditional formats. Accordingly, most teachers reported that the professional development received through the initiative by professional learning specialists helped to increase confidence levels regarding technology use and develop specific skills for choosing appropriate digital content and tools to positively impact student learning (SRI Education, 2018).

The Daggett System for Effective Instruction also addresses the need for teachers to receive professional development that is purposeful and where time is allocated for practice and feedback. "They need time for reflection with their peers in order to make the best practices part of their repertoire of skills . . . Teachers must be supported in continuous growth toward accessing and using the best instructional strategies and integrating technology into lessons" (Daggett, 2014, p. 6).

The Center for Teacher Quality (2014) also has information about professional development approaches that have been deemed effective for impacting the learning environment. They, too, talk about the need for teacher empowerment and the greater opportunity for collaboration. Recommendations from the Center include that leaders should examine the time teachers have for collaboration. While providing more time would be nice, look first at the structure of the currently available time. Leaders should make sure that the blocks of time are not too short or disjointed in a way that does not support collaboration. The Center also recommends that opportunities are provided for teachers to learn from one another. Trusting teachers to help one another grow leads to increased collaboration and mentoring time.

Finally, the Center suggests looking for ways to expand professional learning offerings and access points so that it is available 24/7 and on mobile devices. Rodman (2018) discusses how Twitter and Voxer chats along with platforms such as virtual book clubs, blogs, and discussion boards are ways that teachers can personalize their own professional learning. One key element of all of these (besides accessibility) is that each includes a social component where teachers can build relationships with other educators to include a global collaborative. Rodman (2018) recommends that "school leaders need to design learning spaces that better support the complete learning loop—spaces in which participants are not just consumers but also producers, co-constructing exceptional instructional designs together" (p.17)

Lamkin and Nesloney (2018) recommend increasing the use of teacher-led video reflection for professional growth. According to the authors, "allowing teachers to choose how they utilize video to meet their own goals and needs could be the single most important component in integrating video into professional learning" (p. 54). Martinelle adds another layer to this approach through the use of video-stimulated recall (VSR) where a facilitator interacting with teachers who are watching video clips of themselves teaching. The periodic stopping of the video to ask the teacher what they were thinking at a given point in the lesson can create powerful conversations. "Good VSR sessions create ideal conditions for reflective conversations between professionals, rather than teacher critiques or coaching sessions" (Martinelle, 2018, p. 55).

According to Hirsch and Hord (2018), "studying with and from peers has been shown to be a powerful learning design" (p. 1). It is clear that faculty can learn a tremendous amount from each other. There are keys practices that should be in place to ensure a successful implementation and include clearly communicating the new vision, the plan to attain the new vision, the professional development to attain the vision, and the assistance necessary to successfully integrate the new technology and associated strategies.

Sheehy and Ceballos (2018) looked at a model of professional learning where teachers would observe each other teaching and give each other feedback. In this model, the teacher getting observed would share for what s/he would like feedback. Observations were reciprocal so that both teachers had time to observe the other *and* give helpful feedback. This model could easily work in a school *if* the teachers were willing to participate *and* if time could be built into the schedule to facilitate this collaboration. The focus could be the technology tool or strategy s/he was learning how to apply.

TECHNOLOGY STANDARDS

Just as there are professional development standards used to guide the work of providers of professional development, there are technology standards that will help with technology integration. These are published through the International Society for Technology Education (ISTE).

The ISTE Standards for Education Leaders as well as the Essential Conditions are identified by ISTE for successful integration of technology. According to ISTE, "The ISTE Standards for Education Leaders support the implementation of the ISTE Standards for Students and the ISTE Standards for Educators and provide a framework for guiding digital age learning. These standards target the knowledge and behaviors required for leaders to empower teachers and make student learning possible" (2020, Standards for Leaders section). "The ISTE Essential Conditions are the 14 essential elements necessary to effectively leverage technology for learning. They offer educators and school leaders a research backed framework to guide implementation of the ISTE Standards, tech planning and system wide change" (ISTE, 2020, Essential Conditions section).

One of the critical elements relates to ongoing professional learning and dedicated time to practice and share ideas. In a review of the standards, it is evident that standard #3, Empowering Leader, focused on enriching learning opportunities by empowering teachers to "exercise professional agency . . . and pursue personalize professional learning." (ISTE, 2020) Leaders should "inspire a culture of innovation" regarding the use of digital tools (ISTE, 2020).

MODELS OF PROFESSIONAL DEVELOPMENT FOR TECHNOLOGY

While many elements of professional development apply for all forms of professional development opportunities, there are some unique needs that should be addressed with professional development for technology integration.

SAMR

The SAMR is an approach that can be used by K-12 educators to select, use and evaluate technology. SAMR is an acronym that stands for

Substitution: Tech acts as a direct tool substitute, with no functional change
Augmentation: Tech acts as a direct tool substitute, with functional improvement

Modification: Tech allows for significant task redesign
Redefinition: Tech allows for the creation of new tasks, previously inconceivable (Hamilton et al., 2016, p. 434)

A quick Google search of SAMR will provide many different representations of this model. Think of this as a four-step ladder. The first two steps represent a level of technology integration and *enhanced* current classroom practices. The second two steps represent a higher level of technology integration that has the potential to *transform* the learning experiences (Hamilton et al., 2016).

It is important to pay attention to the SAMR model when planning technology professional development. In a study that examined the integration of iPads, the researchers noted that lack of technical support and time for professional development were identified as central reasons for why or why not a program may fail. "A top-down, hardware driven approach failed to support instructional pedagogy and student learning. We argue that technology can be an integral part of solving challenges in teacher instruction or practice; however, technology use should be predicated in the instructional problem of practice" (Zinger et al., 2019, p. 3).

CONCLUSION

As Jenn Smith wrapped up her investigation and thought about how she planned to present this information to her leadership team, she ran across one quote that spoke volumes. "Most initiatives are sprinkled onto us, but the best sort of change must come from us" (Hill, 2019). Jenn chose to open her leadership meeting with this quote and ask her team members what it meant to them. Then she summarized her findings and asked for input on how well constructed professional learning opportunities would help the faculty learn how to effectively employ the digital tools they had available.

Her committee identified themes from the literature review that Jenn had conducted. Next, they discussed the development of a plan that could be an offshoot of a lesson study approach as well as dedicated times where "experts" could showcase one way they were successfully implementing a digital tool. The committee also, based upon the research completed, suggested that a subcommittee come together to determine how the master schedule could be adjusted to accommodate more team level planning time. However, through all of the dialogue many members expressed concern about how to ensure that the implementation actually worked this time. Many were fearful that some teachers would be unwilling to give technology integration a fresh start.

Based upon this information, Jenn and her committee determine a plan of action that includes time allocated for collaboration, the sharing of ideas and time for the teachers to gain insight into the new "vision" for the school and how exciting learning opportunities with technology can be for the students. They decide first to create a showcase of successes with other schools that have taken a similar path. Next, they created a showcase of successes within the faculty, highlighting those who have been integrating technology with great success. In professional learning communities (PLC), the teachers determine that they will take on one strategy a month. First, they will learn about it in a PLC meeting. The next week, they will brainstorm ways to use it in their classrooms, the third week they will come together to talk about what worked and what did not and what to do about it and to go on a walk about to see how other teachers implement it. Finally, on the fourth week, they will come together as PLCs to celebrate success. Then the cycle will start again with a focus on a new tool.

As a result of this plan, Jenn and her assistant principal will focus their classroom walkthroughs each month on the technology tool chosen so that they can provide feed forward to help each teacher to be successful. The progress made through weekly walk throughs and feedback will help teacher to monitor their own progress.

REFLECT AND APPLY ACTIVITIES

8.1 How can administrators and teacher leaders address the barriers that stand in the way of job-embedded, professional learning programs in schools? Which of these barriers are evident in your specific location and how could these be addressed?

8.2 In what ways could opportunities for collaboration and just-in-time professional learning change the way teachers perceive most professional development? How could collaboration and just-in-time professional development be offered at your location?

REFERENCES

Center for Teaching Quality. (2014). *A Global Network of Teachers and their Professional Learning Systems.* http://www.teachingquality.org/wpcontent/uploads/2019/09/CTQ_Global_TeacherSolutions_Report_Professional_Learning_Systems_07112014.pdf.

Chacko, T. (2018). Emerging pedagogies for effective adult learning: From andragogy to heutagogy. *Archives of Medicine and Health Sciences, 6*(2), 278.

Daggett, W. (2014). *The Daggett System for Effective Instruction.* International Center for Leadership in Education. https://leadered.com/wp-content/uploads/Daggett_System_for_Effective_Instruction_2014.pdf.

Hamilton, E., Rosenberg, J., & Akcaoglu, M. (2016, May 28). The substitution, augmentation, modification, redefinition (SAMR) model: A critical review and suggestions for its use. *TechTrends, 60,* 433–441.

Heick, T. (2018). The difference between pedagogy, andragogy and heutagogy. *Teachthought.* https://www.teachthought.com/pedagogy/a-primer-in-heutagogy-and-self-directed-learning/.

Hill, L. (2019). Upside down is right side up: Shifting priorities for professional learning. *Center for Teaching Quality.* https://www.teachingquality.org/upside-down-is-right-side-up-shifting-priorities-for-professional-learning-lauren-hill/.

Hirsch, S., & Hord, S. (2018). Great plan, disappointing results: Managing implementation is critical. *Tools for Learning Schools, 21*(2). https://learningforward.org/tools-for-learning-schools/spring-2018-vol-21-no-2/.

International Society for Technology Education. (2020). *Standards for Education Leaders.* https://www.iste.org/standards/for-education-leaders.

International Society for Technology Education. (2020). *Essential Conditions.* https://www.iste.org/standards/essential-conditions.

Lamkin, S., & Nesloney, T. (2018). Spreading the practice of video reflection. *Educational Leadership, 73*(3), 50–54.

Learning Forward. (2011). *Standards for Professional Learning.* https://learningforward.org/standards/.

Martinelle, R. (2018). Video-Stimulated recall: Aiding teacher practice. *Educational Leadership, 73*(3), 55.

Psiropoulos, D., Barr, S., Eriksson, C., Fletcher, S., Hargis, J., & Cavanaugh, C. (2016, March 7). Professional development for iPad integration in general education: Staying ahead of the curve. *Education and Information Technology, 21,* 209–228.

Rodman, A. (2018). Learning together, learning on their own. *Educational Leadership, 73*(3), 12–18.

Sheehy, K., & Ceballos, L. (2018). The expert next door: Lesson observations and peer feedback. *Tools for Learning Schools, 21*(3). https://learningforw ard.org/tools-for-learning-schools/summer-2018-vol-21-no-3-2/.

SRI Education. (2018). *The Apple and ConnectED initiative: Baseline and Year 2 Findings from Principal, Teacher and Student Surveys.* www.sri.com /education.

Zinger, D., Tate, T., & Warschnauer, M. (2019). Learning and teaching with technology: Technological pedagogy and teacher practice. In *The SAGE Handbook for Research on Teacher Education.* SAGE Publications.

Chapter 9

Technology Coaches

Lin Carver

Ralph Sanchez arrived before the staff on his first day as the principal of Sumpter Middle School. Since this was a school where he had not had the opportunity to spend much time before being assigned as principal, he was anxious to get a closer look at what was happening in the classrooms. He knew that the school grade had dropped from a C to a D this past year, so he was a little concerned about what he might find.

Upon arriving in his office, the first thing he did was to open his computer. Using the internet, he retrieved a map of the school that indicated the teacher and grade level of each classroom. As he did this, he was pleased to notice that the wireless network seemed to be robust and reliable. The routers were working well, and the computer was a current version. Then he spent the next couple of minutes checking his email and searching the web. With the immediate concerns taken care of, he still had a few minutes left before school started so he made his way to the classrooms. He was thrilled with what he saw there. Most of the classrooms contained interactive whiteboards, multiple laptops, and various mobile devices. He took a moment to open one of the laptops and explore the programs available for student use. The technology and software programs appeared to be abundant and readily available. He could not wait to see how the faculty integrated all these digital resources into their instruction.

Since the faculty and students were beginning to arrive, Ralph made rounds introducing himself to everyone. He enjoyed getting to meet everyone; they seemed cordial and friendly. When the starting bell rang at 9:00 am, he made time to visit the classrooms to see instruction as it was occurring in fifteen of the twenty-five classrooms. By the time he returned to his office, he was depressed. In every room in which he observed, the technology sat on the shelves unused. At this rate the technology would be buried in dust by the end of the school year, he thought. During instruction, the students had sat at individual desks quietly completing worksheets or independently reading their textbooks. This was a problem!

After careful deliberation, he decided that his first goal would be to address instructional practices and student engagement. After contemplating the issue, he decided it would be helpful to hire an instructional technology coach. The technology was available, but teachers were not using it to engage students or increase student achievement. He needed someone to help the faculty move to the next level of technology integration. Since he did not have a technology instructional coach, he pondered exactly what he should look for in a coach and what he wanted the coach to be able to do. What skillset should the coach have, he wondered? He started to make a list. He would use that list to help create the ad for the new position.

ROLE OF TECHNOLOGY

Ralph Sanchez was concerned about the lack of technology integration during instruction. Research studies have found that the integration of technology into instruction has the potential to transform learning. Today's students use digital technologies frequently; however, often their use is limited to social networking and internet searches (Thompson, 2013). For students to develop sophisticated uses of digital technology, these uses need to be explicitly integrated into their learning. Darling-Hammond, Zielezinski, and Goldman (2014) determined that "significant gains in achievement and engagement can occur for underserved students in learning environments characterized by computer use that engages students in interactive learning that offers multiple representations of ideas and real-time digital feedback" (p. 10). Just having access to technology is not enough. Darling-Hammond et al. (2014) determined that "teacher assistance seems to be mandatory for the online learning" (p. 12).

However, many teachers either don't have the time or are resistant to using technology in the classroom. In fact, despite significant investment and technology policy initiatives, there have not been significant changes in how instruction occurs (Howard & Mozejko, 2015). So, we come back to Ralph Sanchez's concern, how do we impact teachers' technology usage?

There are three key factors that significantly impact teachers' use of digital technologies and result in changes in instructors' teaching and students' learning: (1) leadership, (2) shared group vision, and (3) technical and pedagogical support. The first factor, leadership, relates to the actions and attitudes of the school administrative team. The way in which the administration prioritizes digital technologies had the strongest impact on teachers' use and related student-centered pedagogy (Law et al., 2008). An important component to consider when prioritizing technology usage is the development of a clear vision of how digital technologies are expected to be implemented into instruction. Including teachers in the creation of this vision leads to the second key point. By participating in the creation of a "shared vision," teachers are more likely to feel more invested in technology use and change. This process helps to create a school culture for change (Howard & Mozejko, 2015, p. 7). In order for a significant change in technology integration to occur, teachers need to be able to take risks and experiment with how they design learning tasks and classroom interactions. Incorporating these components creates an environment for change that has a community focus rather than being the responsibility of each individual teacher.

When technology is integrated into the curriculum it revolutionizes the learning process. Technology integration in the curriculum improves students' learning. Teachers who use computers as tools for problem-solving change the way they teach. This change in emphasis tends to move teachers from a behavioral approach to a more constructivist approach (Edutopia, 2015). However, it is important to consider what is meant by technology integration. Edutopia (2007) defines classroom technology integration as "more than teaching basic computer skills and software programs in a separate computer class. Effective tech integration must happen across the curriculum in ways that research shows deepen and enhance the learning process. In particular, it must support four key components of learning: active engagement, participation in groups, frequent interaction and feedback, and connection to real-world experts" (para. 3).

THEORETICAL BACKGROUND
ABOUT COACHING

To help to bring about change in instructional practices in Sumpter Middle School, Ralph Sanchez was considering hiring a technology instructional coach. Knight (2016) describes instructional coaches as individuals who partner with "teachers to help them improve teaching and learning so students are more successful" (para.1). To encourage collaboration between the coach and teachers, the instructional coach typically has a nonsupervisory, nonevaluative role. Instead of operating from a position of power, instructional coaches use their expertise and relationship to help bring about change (Taylor, 2008).

The focus of instructional coaching is on the content or curricular instruction with the goal of supporting school or district instructional reform (Mangin & Stoelinga, 2008; Neufeld & Roper, 2002). Because of the increased emphasis on student achievement nation-wide, these reform efforts over the past few decades have focused on improving content-based instructional practice (Elmore, 2004).

Teachers, who move into the role of instructional coach, are often viewed as sharing leadership for instructional reform with the administrative team (Taylor, 2008). In this role, there is evidence that coaches can act as mediators between district- or school-initiated reform efforts and teachers' classroom practice (Hubbard et al., 2006).

However, just because a teacher is proficient with technology does not mean that the teacher will be an effective technology coach. Effective coaching begins with an understanding of the school's context and goals. In addition, coaches must also be able to increase other teachers' confidence, knowledge, and skills through productive conversations, modeling, and support. Technology instructional coaches must have a desire to provide other teachers with both instructional and technical support. They need to understand that technology can be used to support teaching and learning, but that technology alone is not the whole solution (Swinnerton, 2007).

CHARACTERISTICS OF COACHES

Various researchers have created lists of coaching characteristics. Knight (2006) indicated that coaching requires skills in communication, relationship building, change management, and leadership for teacher professional development. *PBWorks* (2007) more specifically describes the skills of communication by indicating the importance of the coach's ability to express content expertise based upon teaching experience and expertise. It more specifically describes relationship building as a component of coaching skills. *PBWorks* (2007) expands the coaching skills into six categories: content expertise, teaching expertise, beliefs, relationship skills, coaching, and leadership skills. They further explained each of these six skills; however, they did not address the coach's need for an understanding of change management which is an important characteristic.

Teaching expertise is further described as experience in instructional planning, establishing classroom management and organizational systems, easily using multiple methods of assessment and instruction, and being reflective practitioners.

PBWorks (2007) clearly identified some of the beliefs that coaches need to possess. These beliefs begin with the growth mindset that teachers hold about their students, but these beliefs also expand to include having a growth mindset about themselves and other teachers. Coaches need to be willing to learn, need to believe that everyone has an important role to play in the instructional process, and that everyone is capable of growing. Coaches need to be passionate about growth while not assuming they have "the Answer." The coach's goal should be for all teachers to be the most effective teachers they can be.

The area of leadership skills encompasses an understanding of adults as learners. Coaches need to be skillful listeners who are able to understand teachers' concerns, communicate effectively, understand adult learning principles, diagnose teacher's needs, and provide appropriate support to help teachers meet those needs (Carver & Orth, 2017).

ADVERTISING FOR AN INSTRUCTIONAL TECHNOLOGY COACH

So, when looking for a technology coach, what are the characteristics Ralph Sanchez should look for? Which are the criteria he should consider listing in the job description?

An instructional technology coach should be a certified teacher who can support the implementation of instructional programs, provide staff development, and coach teachers on the integration of technology into instruction in literacy, mathematics, and other content areas. The typical instruction coach needs to be able to perform a variety of duties. Some of the responsibilities might include

- Support the implementation of school goals for curricular programs and technology
- Provide staff development for technology integration to support learning
- Train faculty in digital tools for creation, exploration, and interaction
- Model strategies and technology for teachers
- Assist with selection and implementation of new digital resources
- Facilitate technology troubleshooting

In order to employ individuals who are prepared to accomplish these items, it will be important for Ralph Sanchez to identify the required and preferred qualifications in his advertisement.

This advertisement should probably begin with the basic qualifications of a valid teaching certificate with a minimum of three to five years of teaching experience at the level at which the coach would be providing support. In addition, the potential coach should have evidence of proficient teaching with technology through demonstration, portfolio, or course work.

Preferred qualifications might include: experience facilitating workshops, demonstrating lessons, and analyzing and using data to inform decisions. It would also be helpful for the candidate to have extensive leadership in staff development, effective oral and written communication skills, and knowledge of current theories, techniques, and methodologies related to instruction and technology integration. The candidate should also be an advocate for incorporating ideas related to digital citizenship (ISTE, 2019).

ESTABLISHING THE COACHING PROCESS

Supporting teachers is the goal of any instructional coaching program. However, to accomplish this there is not one single magic program to follow that will meet the needs of all teachers. A one-size-fits-all approach to technology integration does not work. Coaches instead should enter into a collaborative cycle of support through goal setting, co-planning, observation, and reflection with individual teachers. The coaching program should be built on the connections with teachers related to technology. Because teachers may not take the first step in reaching out to the coach often due to a lack of knowledge about the options available, coaches must reach out to teachers. These connections will enable the coach to understand where teachers are feeling confident as well as the challenges they are facing. An effective first step is for the coach to informally visit the classrooms. After visiting the classroom, the coach can leave positive messages recognizing the teacher's abilities and willingness to take risks. This step will help the teacher to feel affirmed by the coach and to perceive working with the coach as a non-threatening opportunity. These classroom visits will help the coach to see the types of teacher-student interactions and to understand what technology would most enhance the individual teacher's style and instruction.

The first meeting of the coaching cycle typically begins with the teacher and the coach discussing how technology could be used to support the content or standards. The analysis of the instructional content is the starting point. Based on the content goal, technology could be identified that would enhance the unit, lesson plan, curriculum, or assessment. Joseph and Fisher (2018) created a list of questions to consider when integrating technology to create relevant and authentic learning opportunities.

- What is the goal the teacher wants to accomplish?
- Why would the use of technology be helpful in this setting?
- How will the use of technology enhance the current instruction?
- Will the use of technology make this idea more relevant to the students?
- Will adding technology enable the students to accomplish something they could not have done without it?

Sometimes it might be helpful to work backward by identifying the goal first and then deciding the most effective way to accomplish that goal. Conclude the meeting by establishing the next steps so that the action plan is clear to both the teacher and the coach.

The next step would be the implementation of the plan that was developed. This might include having the coach model or co-teach to illustrate the implementation of the technology that was identified in the plan. Although the coach brings information about digital resources, the classroom teacher is the content area expert. The goal is for the teacher to see the technology in use without having to worry about implementing it on his own.

Following the lesson, the teacher and coach should reflect on the effectiveness of the tools that were implemented, how easy or hard they were to use, and any problems or areas of difficulty that will need to be addressed. These reflective notes help to document what tools were used and they provide a tangible record for the teacher to refer back to when planning other lessons.

Now it is time for the teacher to use the new tools or skills independently. After the teacher has used the tools or skills independently, the coach should meet with the teacher to discuss additional concerns or questions that may have developed. It is important at this stage to reflect with the teacher about what went well and what might need to be improved upon. Once the teacher is feeling comfortable implementing the technology, the coach should revisit the classroom to see how it is going or whether the teacher is ready to implement additional resources. This would be a great opportunity to also check with the students about their reactions to the new resources. Then it is time to start a new coaching cycle (Joseph & Fisher, 2018).

EVALUATING TECHNOLOGY INTEGRATION

Sometimes teachers will use technology for technology's sake rather than evaluating when and how technology should be used. Guymon (2014) has identified five steps for evaluating technology integration. The first step in determining the need involves identifying the most important area of need and identifying a tool to meet that need. The rubric in table 9.1 might be helpful in identifying the specific area of need and the extent to which that tool meets the identified need.

After the most important need has been determined and a possible tool to meet that need has been identified, the second step would be to develop a goal statement for the objective to be accomplished (Guymon, 2014). The chart in table 9.2 can be used to identify the components of the goal statement. The more specific the goal is, the easier it will be to tell if the identified tool is helping to meet this goal.

Table 9.1   Evaluating Technology Integration

Identified Area of Need	None	Some & Tool	Significant & Tool
Student achievement			
Student engagement			
School policy			
New expectations			
Other: Specify			

Table 9.2   SMART Goal

	Skill to be Developed (S)	Method for Measuring Demonstration of the Skill (M)	Proficiency Level (A)	Proficiency Percentage Goal (R)	Length of Time Needed (T)
Example-	3-minute web 2.0 video on mitosis	rubric	4.0	80%	End of the first quarter
SMART Goal Components					

When developing the goal statement, a goal that is written as a SMART goal helps the teacher decide if the specific goal has been met. The format of the SMART goal is particularly helpful. A SMART goal will be clear and obtainable if each component of SMART is addressed: Specific (what do you want the students to be able to accomplish), Measurable (how will you know if the students have reached this goal), Achievable (at what level should the students be able to demonstrate the skill), Realistic (what percentage of students should be able to demonstrate this skill at this level), and Time-bound (in what period of time should it be accomplished) (Eby, 2019). The pieces of a SMART goal are illustrated in table 9.2.

The pieces from table 9.2 can be combined into a single sentence. The following SMART goal could be created: By the end of the first quarter, 80 percent of the eighth-grade students at Paul R. Smith Middle School will demonstrate the ability to create a three-minute, web 2.0 video on mitosis and score at least a 4.0 on the rubric.

Now that the need has been determined and the SMART goal has been developed, it is important to design appropriate instruction (Guymon,

Table 9.3   Digital Tool Considerations

	Readiness Level	Physical Skills Needed	Methods of Instruction	Length of Time Needed
Designing Instruction				

2014). When designing the instruction, it will be important to identify the students' readiness level, their current physical skill level, and their engagement level. These will be important considerations when preparing students to interact with the new tool or digital resource. Table 9.3 can be used to organize these considerations.

When designing the instruction, it will also be important to consider the instructional environment. Think about the classroom layout and available materials. Determine how these can best be arranged to meet the SMART goal. Don't forget to develop a backup plan for those students who are not successful the first time the information is presented.

Often the final step is forgotten. This is probably one of the most important steps. Go back to the goal statement and analyze the results. What does the data show? Consider whether your goal was met, whether the goal needs to be revised, or whether the tool accomplished what it was supposed to accomplish. The tool might be effective, or it might not be as effective as you hoped it would be. Your expectations might not have been realistic. Or you might need to go back to the drawing board and start over again.

CONCLUSION

As has been evident in each of the chapters throughout the book, administrative leadership (district leadership, principals, assistant principals, coaches, and lead teachers) can make a significant difference in the effectiveness of technology integration to support academic achievement for all learners. The question to be considered is not if technology is used. The question is not even at which of the SAMR levels is the technology used. The important question is how does the technology that is used help to improve student academic achievement and critical thinking. This should be the guiding focus of all technology integration.

REFLECT AND APPLY ACTIVITIES

9.1 Based on the information in this chapter, your personal experience, and other scholarly resources, develop a Help Wanted Ad for Ralph Sanchez to use when advertising for an Instructional Technology Coach. Make sure to include the Major Duties and Responsibilities, Required Qualifications, and Desired Qualifications.

9.2 Talk to an instructional coach and have the coach generate a list of the characteristics that are important for a coach to demonstrate. Evaluate your strengths. How do your strengths compare to those identified by the coach? Identify one area where you would like to expand your skills. Develop a SMART goal for helping you grow in one specific area.

REFERENCES

Carver, L., & Orth, J. (2017). *Coaching: Making a Difference for K-12 Students and Teachers.* Lanham, MD: Rowman & Littlefield.

Darling-Hammond, L., Zielezinski, M. B., & Goldman, S. (2014). *Using Technology to Support At-Risk Students' Learning.* Alliance for Excellent Education and Stanford Center for Opportunity Policy in Education.

Eby, K. (2019, January 9). *The Essential Guide to Writing SMART Goals.* https://www.smartsheet.com/blog/essential-guide-writing-smart-goals.

Edutopia. (2015, June 23). Making technology work. https://www.edutopia.org/practice/instructional-coaching-driving-meaningful-tech-integration.

Edutopia. (2007, November 5). Why do we need technology integration? https://www.edutopia.org/technology-integration-guide-importance.

Elmore, R. F. (2004). *School Reform from the Inside Out: Policy, Practice, and Performance.* Harvard Education Press.

Guymon, D. (2014, February 13). The 5 steps of effective technology integration. *Getting Smart.* https://www.gettingsmart.com/2014/02/5-steps-effective-technology-integration/.

Howard, S. K., & Mozejko, A. (2015). *Teachers: Technology, Change and Resistance.* University of Wollongong Research Online. https://pdfs.semanticscholar.org/317f/2ec69c476757655a6a350fcabeb876c6c817.pdf.

Hubbard, L., Mehan, H., & Stein, M. K. (2006). *Reform as Learning: School Reform, Organizational Culture, and Community Politics in San Diego.* Routledge.

ISTE. (2019). ISTE standards for coaches. *International Society for Technology in Education.* https://www.iste.org/standards/for-coaches.

Joseph, M. X., & Fisher, E. (2018, June 4). The 6 fundamentals of technology coaching. *Ed Tech Magazine.* https://edtechmagazine.com/k12/article/2018/06/6-fundamentals-technology-coaching.

Knight, J. (2004). Instructional coaches make progress through partnership: Intensive support can improve teaching. *Journal of Staff Development, 25*(2), 32–37.

Knight, J. (2016). What do instructional coaches do? *Instructional Coaching Group.* https://www.instructionalcoaching.com/what-do-instructional-coaches-do/.

Law, N., Pelgrum, W. J., & Plomp, T. (2008). *Pedagogy and ICT Use in School Around the World: Findings from the IEA SITES 2006 Study.* Comparative Education Research Centre (CERC) and Springer.

Mangin, M. M., & Stoelinga, S. R. (2008). Teacher leadership: What it is and why it matters. In M. M. Mangin & S. R. Stoelinga (Eds.), *Effective Teacher Leadership: Using Research to Inform and Reform* (pp. 10–35). Teachers College Press.

Neufeld, B., & Roper, D. (2002). *Off to a Good Start: Year I of Collaborative Coaching and Learning in the Effective Practice Schools.* Education Matters, Inc.

PBWorks. (2007). Being an effective coach. http://coaches.pbworks.com/w/page/7518652/Becoming%20an%20Effective%20Coach.

Swinnerton, J. (2007). Brokers and boundary crossers in an urban school district: Understanding central office coaches as instructional leaders. *Journal of School Leadership, 17*(2), 195–221.

Taylor, J. E. (2008). Instructional coaching: The state of the art. In M. M. Mangin & S. R. Stoelinga (Eds.), *Effective Teacher Leadership: Using Research to Inform and Reform* (pp. 10–35). Teachers College Press.

Thompson, P. (2013). The digital natives as learners: Technology use patterns and approaches to learning. *Computers & Education, 65,* 12–33. doi:10.1016/j.compedu.2012.12.022.

Index

Author Bios

Holly Atkins, PhD
Holly Atkins earned her BA, MEd, and PhD in Curriculum and Instruction from the University of South Florida. Prior to arriving at Saint Leo University, she worked as a middle grades English/Language arts teacher. She is an associate professor of Education, the chair of the Undergraduate Education Department, and director of the Teacher Technology Summer Institute at Saint Leo University. Dr. Atkins has engaged in over fifty presentations and publications focusing on the meaningful use of technology in education.

Lin Carver, PhD
Lin Carver joined Saint Leo University with over thirty years of experience as a teacher and administrator in K-12 schools (teacher, coach, and director), and as an adjunct professor at various universities prior to joining the Saint Leo University community. She currently serves as the director of Program Approval in the College of Education and Social Services and the program administrator for the Master's in Reading Program. Her teaching responsibilities are in Graduate Studies in Education in the Reading, ESE, Instructional Leadership, and Education Doctorate programs. Her presentations, publications, and research focus on increasing student achievement through effective literacy instruction, engagement, technology, and educational interventions.

Alexandra Kanellis, PhD
Alexandra Kanellis, a former special education teacher and associate chair of the undergraduate education program, has been in teacher preparation for more than a decade focusing on special education, assessment, technology. and classroom management. She has offered professional development to private and public schools nationally and internationally.

Jodi Lamb, PhD
Jodi Lamb earned a BA in English Education, MS in Library Science and a PhD in Curriculum and Instruction from the University of South Florida. Prior to arriving at Saint Leo, Dr. Jodi Lamb spent over twenty-eight years working in three different public schools districts and held positions that ranged from media specialist to staff developer to principal. She served as a school or district administrator for sixteen years. She worked at all levels K-12, both traditional and alternative, and served as an adjunct in graduate education for several universities before coming to Saint Leo University full-time. Dr. Lamb teaches in the educational leadership, instructional leadership and Ed.S/Ed.D. programs. She is the program administrator for the educational leadership and instructional leadership programs and the associate director for the Graduate Studies in Education department.

Keya Mukherjee, PhD
Keya Mukherjee received her PhD from the University of South Florida in Curriculum and Instruction in Applied Linguistics and Instructional Technology/Instructional Design. In addition to teaching in higher education, she has taught adult ESL students and trained teachers in the United States as well as international contexts. She is the program administrator for the ESOL and Instructional Design programs at Saint Leo University where she designs, develops, and currently teaches courses on instructional design, ESOL, diversity and multicultural education, and research methodology. Her current research interests are specifically on teaching innovation in online learning, culturally sensitive online pedagogy, and student engagement.

Lauren Pantoja, MEd
Lauren Pantoja is a learning design coach at Paul R. Smith Middle School in Pasco County, Florida, where she supports teachers in

technology and literacy in all contents. She earned a masters from Webster University which she has used during her more than thirty years as a K-12 educator and coach. She also designs and teaches courses for Pasco County School District to support teachers, and works as an adjunct instructor at Saint Leo University preparing future literacy teachers and coaches. These experiences provide the foundation which has resulted in her recognition as Florida Literacy Coach of the Year.

Tammy Quick, PhD
Tammy Quick is an assistant professor of Undergraduate Education at Saint Leo University. She received a BA in Elementary Education K-6, and her MEd in Reading K-12 from Saint Leo University. Dr. Quick earned her PhD in Early Childhood Education at Florida State University. Dr. Quick has twenty-five years of classroom experience in the private and public sector. She is the program administrator for Educational Studies, Early Childhood Development and Education program at Saint Leo University. Dr. Quick's research interests include literacy instruction, STR2EAM, and technology in P-12 education.

Donna Reeves-Brown, PhD candidate
Donna Reeves-Brown is a doctoral candidate at the University of Kentucky in Educational Leadership with a focus on School Technology Leadership. At present, Reeves-Brown is the technology curriculum consultant for the Archdiocese of Louisville Catholic Schools and an adjunct at Bellarmine University. Prior to working at the archdiocese, she was a high school mathematics and computer science teacher in public schools.

Georgina Rivera-Singletary, PhD
Georgina Rivera-Singletary is associate professor for graduate studies in Special Education at Saint Leo University. Dr. Rivera-Singletary has twenty years experience in K-12 public school with roles in school and district administration, migrant resource teacher, alternative education, adult education, ESOL adult education instructor, and high school foreign language classrooms. She also worked with the Puerto Rico Department of Education secretary of education's office providing technical assistance for RTI, ELL, PLC, and teacher evaluation processes and programs. Her research interests include special populations, social justice, and policy for migrant students with disabilities and English learners.

Kevin Thomas, PhD
Kevin Thomas is a professor at Bellarmine University. Prior to entering higher education, Dr. Thomas taught high school English for fifteen years in Tennessee. His research examines teacher and student perceptions regarding the instructional benefits and barriers related to the classroom integration of personal mobile devices. Additional research interests include exploration of the use of Web 2.0 tools to expand the traditional boundaries associated with the classroom through online interaction, and dispositional and racial issues in teacher preparation programs.